REAL ESTATE INVESTING

NOTHING HELD BACK

NELYA CALEV

Copyright © 2023 Nelya and Joseph Calev

All rights reserved. This book or parts thereof may not be reproduced in any form, stored in any retrieval system, or transmitted in any form by any means—electronic, mechanical, photocopy, recording, or otherwise—without prior written permission of the author, except as provided by United States of America copyright law. For permission requests write to the author, addressed "Attention: Permissions Coordinator," at the address found at the social media below.

ISBN: 978-1-7362617-4-3 (Paperback)

Library of Congress Control Number: 2023901554

Limit of liability: Please note that much of this publication is based on personal experience and anecdotal evidence. Although the author has made every reasonable attempt to achieve complete accuracy of the content in this book, she makes no representations or warranties with respect to the accuracy or completeness of the contents of this book and specifically disclaims any implied warranties of merchantability or fitness for a particular purpose. Your particular circumstances may not be suited to the examples illustrated in this book and in fact they likely will not be. You should use the information in this book at your own risk. Nothing in this book is intended to replace common sense or legal, accounting, or professional advice, and is meant only to inform.

First edition 2023

Publisher:

Nelya Calev

Bellevue, WA

Book design by Sofia Krasnovskaya.

Instagram: @nelyac

Contents

Preface: Who This Book Is For v
Chapter 1: Our Story 1
Chapter 2: Decision Making 9
Chapter 3: Building Relationships 17
Chapter 4: Networking 27
Chapter 5: Math Stuff 33
Chapter 6: Types of Investing 53
Chapter 7: Rapid Decisions 65
Chapter 8: Identifying Properties 77
Chapter 9: The Contract 85
Chapter 10: Due Diligence 95
Chapter 11: Working with Banks 103
Chapter 12: Working with Partners 119
Chapter 13: Self-Managing Properties 129
Chapter 14: Property Managers 141
Chapter 15: Utilities 149
Chapter 16: Death and Taxes 155
Chapter 17: Closing the Deal 167
Chapter 18: The Value Add 173
Chapter 19: Building Maintenance 181
Chapter 20: Figuring Stuff Out 191
Chapter 21: Mental State 197

Preface
Who This Book Is For

It was December of 2012 and the entire metropolitan area of Seattle had been covered by several inches of shimmering snow. The city, whose landscape is tremendously hilly and packed with over three million people completely unfamiliar with this puffy white stuff, was paralyzed. Few cars dared face the unplowed roads and the populace prepared to do what they always did for that once-every-few-years snowstorm: they waited patiently at home for it to melt.

In one of the many suburbs that had shut down, on a small crest in a working-class neighborhood not far from the freeway, stood a duplex. It was unspectacular and, unluckily for the sellers, had been listed for sale a few days before. I'm not sure how many people noticed this duplex, but I did. So I asked our neighbor to watch our kids for a few hours and had my husband, Joseph, who grew up in a snowy area of the Northeast, drive me to see it.

The duplex was a nondescript building not more than twelve hundred square feet in total. It had paper-thin walls, a post-and-pier foundation, and was so flimsy that a good wind would carry it away. Upon seeing it, I looked at my husband and declared, "What a piece of shit! I want it!"

Over the last few years we'd scraped together barely $20,000. We had just enough for the down payment and nothing for the repairs, but we didn't care. Miraculously, because no one else dared to trudge out in the snow, we got it for under list price.

Over the next ten years I expanded our real estate business to roughly a hundred times its original size. I started by not knowing what I didn't know and have learned as things went on. I can't say that it's been easy. I've cried and screamed and have had mental breakdowns.

If you bought this book thinking I was going to provide "magic fairy dust" that would lift you into riches, you're gravely mistaken. This business is *difficult*. It will drain you in ways you never thought possible. At various times you'll wonder whether the universe has it out for you, and at others you'll marvel at the incompetence of your fellow human beings. You'll lash out at your family. You'll hang up on your mother. If you're a woman, people will call you a bitch. But maybe, just maybe, if you listen to what I tell you here, you'll at least *succeed*.

Most real estate investors don't succeed. Your friends who invest won't tell you that. After all, who likes to brag about their failures? They'll tell you all about the properties they purchased and about all the money they supposedly made. But when press just gently, you'll also learn that they haven't done another deal in years.

"Oh, it was an amazing success," they'll say, but they won't offer great reasons why they stopped investing.

The bitter truth is, every profession that makes good money isn't easy. Sure, you may be jealous of the huge contract that a professional athlete just signed, but how much does he exercise every day? How many years did she work to get there? How many bones have they broken and painful surgeries have they endured? How many others worked just as hard but didn't make it? If you want to succeed in real estate, you're going to need to work for it. I'll provide you with the tools to get started, but I can't guarantee your success. Only you can do that.

This book isn't intended to be motivational. If you want that, there are a great number of classes where you can shell out tens of thousands of dollars, be awed into greatness for two days, and then return home to accomplish nothing. I'm going to be blunt about this. If you don't do the work, you're not going to win at this game. There are plenty of books and talks that promise to tell you the formula for real estate success. You'll supposedly learn exactly *what* you need to buy and *how* to buy it. Well, guess what? The market changes. For those of you who follow the stock market, do you think any stock I could possibly recommend while writing this book will still be a good buy when you read this? No. That market changes and so does real estate. Most of those courses are out of date by the time of print. I *will* discuss the different options available, but which one is the most profitable will depend on the times.

What this book *will* do is help you on your journey. I'll go through many of the basic terms so you'll sound like less of a newbie when talking to lenders and agents. I'll share with you what mistakes we made and free you to make new ones. I'll show you how to get started in this industry because it's infamously hostile to newcomers. I'll provide you with the right tools to get the job done.

I also hope to put you into the right mindset, because mindset really is the number one reason for success or failure. You need to recognize what you're buying, to whom you're renting it, and what your goals are. You may be surprised to learn that most new investors don't know these things, but I have a feeling once I point out some of them, you'll realize you didn't know either. I'm also not going to sugarcoat reality. This isn't a "You Can Do It" book. It's a detailed manual on the real estate investment business.

Finally, this book most definitely isn't an advertisement. I've read my share of books about various aspects of investing and nothing upsets my stomach more than a sales pitch in the middle.

You've bought my book and I thank you. I don't need more of your money. I mean, if you send me a big check out of the goodness of your heart I won't throw it away, but I'm not going to upsell you my series of videos. There's no "intense training course" you can pay a lot of money for where I personally repeat the same information found in this book.

I'll let you in on a little secret. My properties actually do pretty well for me. I wrote this book because I recognized that a lot of misinformation is out there and I want to set things straight. I do thoroughly believe the content will help you win in real estate.

Now that you know *what* this book is, you're probably wondering if it's the right book for you. How experienced do you need to be for the material? Is this for investors interested in flips or multifamily, or someone who just wants to rent out a condo or two? In truth, I try to cover all the above. That does mean that some of the content will be complicated to the new investor and those readers may want to go through some paragraphs and chapters more than once.

This business can be complicated; I can't hide that. In numerous cases I go into gory details that other books ignore. If you're new to investing, this book *will* help you, but you'll have to take it slow.

In terms of what types of real estate to buy, I've dedicated space to discuss how to match a given real estate type to your goals. That being said, my specialty is multifamily, so you'll find many references to that world. Even so, most of the material is still relevant to those doing flips or just renting out a condo.

So, with those things understood, let's get started!

Chapter 1
Our Story

BEFORE I BEGIN spewing advice, you should get to know me. I was born in what was then the Union of Soviet Socialist Republics. Although I often simplify my origins by saying I'm from Russia, that's not really the truth.

My Upbringing

I grew up in what is now the city of Khujand, Tajikistan. Back then, it was called Leninabad in the Tajik Soviet Socialist Republic. However, I'm neither Tajik nor Russian, but Jewish. Many Americans will find this concept difficult to grasp but, in the USSR, Jewish was an ethnicity. Literally, my passport has "Jew" under nationality. At home, we spoke a little-known language called Bukharian, which is a mixture of Tajik, Hebrew, and Farsi. We also spoke Russian.

My mother worked as a registered nurse and my father managed a factory that made men's clothing. We were well-to-do for the area until, one day, a government official didn't like the fact that my father was Jewish and ran a factory, so he kicked him to the curb.

Chapter 1

After that, to make ends meet, my father sewed suits at home, and he and my brother traveled to the market on weekends to sell them.

Unfortunately, things weren't going well with the Soviet Union. In America, people cheered when it collapsed in 1991, but that wasn't good news for us. We had barely recovered from the war in Afghanistan, where many boys from our town had died. I used to see vans pull up in the market and load up any boys who looked eighteen or older. Twice my mother and I saved a few by hiding them, then sending them home when it was safe.

When the country collapsed, Islamic militants poured into Tajikistan. It became unsafe to go out, especially for women. If they caught a woman without a head scarf outside, they'd hang her by her hair and then burn her alive. This happened to a girl I knew. My uncle's store was destroyed because he was Jewish. People at school followed us around and said we were baby killers who drank kids' blood on Passover.

Meanwhile, basic commodities dried up. We had to wait in line for hours for anything. My job every evening was to get bread. One night I waited in line, but when the bread truck came there wasn't enough. Hundreds of people stampeded forward to get their bread and I fell. People trampled me until a stranger pulled me out of the mess. After that, we made our own bread, which first required sifting bugs from the flour. That worked, but the bread tasted bitter from what we were sure was bug poop.

The new state of Russia wasn't happy with an Islamic state next to them, so they sent in troops to support the Tajik government. A civil war, never mentioned in the United States news, soon broke out. Over a hundred thousand people died and things became unsafe with very little food available. That's when my parents decided it was time to leave.

Coming to America

Jews had been permitted to leave the Soviet Union for several years, but only Israel offered us harbor and my parents were adamant about going to America. My sister had moved there with her husband two years earlier and she sponsored our application. Although we had some assets in the form of ancient rugs, gold, and our house, we couldn't take any of them. The government strip-searched everyone for valuables at the airport.

The night before we left, we learned from a friend that acquaintances planned to murder us and steal the money we'd saved to resettle in America. We paid our neighbor to stay up all night with a shotgun in our living room. None of us slept that night. The next morning, with two suitcases per person, we left for America. I couldn't say goodbye to my friends. We just left. All we had were our clothes, some pots, and cheap silverware.

When we arrived in Seattle, everything was a shock. We lost one of our bags with half our clothes at the airport, but since we didn't speak English, we didn't make a claim. That first morning, I walked down the street and admired how clean everything was. To us, the most impressive things were the grocery stores. The fruits looked handpicked, even fake, and my first question was "Who ate the bad ones?" I couldn't believe that anyone would throw them away.

We immigrated on a refugee status and initially received government assistance for seven months (meaning we were on welfare). About a week after arriving, I went to a grocery store to buy laundry detergent. This was my first outing on my own in America. I asked my sister what to say if anyone asked me questions, and she said the cashier would ask me whether I wanted paper or plastic. When I proudly placed my detergent on the counter with my food stamps, the cashier started blabbing away in English, so I said "paper." She then spoke faster, and I replied "plastic." After a minute of going back and forth on plastic and paper, she took the detergent from me and pointed to the door. When I arrived home, my sister explained that food stamps are for food, not detergent. I promptly marched back to the store, bought gum with my food stamps (gum is food, right?), and then used the change to buy detergent.

It was a challenging adjustment. I wasn't a five-year-old, who can be easily molded into an American. I was already nineteen and, according to my family, should have been married for three years. My parents and relatives depended on me to guide them through this strange country. I still see them at my door every time they receive any letter they don't understand, which is most of their mail.

Getting Started in America

I signed up for English classes at the community college but had difficulty learning in the classroom environment. Back in Tajikistan, I'd actually failed my high school English class. Desperate to learn, I watched TV with subtitles, then wrote the words I didn't know on sticky notes and plastered them around the house.

Meanwhile, my parents found jobs so we didn't have to be on assistance anymore. My father, instead of running a factory, worked in the back of a tailor shop in Seattle. The owner liked his work but couldn't put him up front because he didn't speak English. My mother, who was a registered nurse, washed dishes at a local deli. After she finished, we cleaned houses together for forty dollars a house.

I worked many jobs to help my family. After a year in the country, I started a new job at the Refugee Federation. I taught immigrants and refugees how to open bank accounts, get around, and find jobs. With the money all of us earned and saved for two years, we bought a house.

Marriage to Joe

In 2000, I met my husband, Joe, who at the time, lived in New York. In 2001, he moved to Seattle. He was born in upstate New York and had grown up in America. Our courtship and marriage were awkward for my family. Everyone before me had accepted an arranged marriage. The thought of me picking my own husband was strange to them, though Joe made things easier by following some of our customs such as asking my parents for my hand and providing a dowry.

His family operated under the traditional model of studying at the best school possible, then working at a high-paying job. The more money one earned, the more one could spend. He had followed that advice well and had studied at Duke University, then started in the software industry.

A few years after Joe and I married, I became an esthetician at a prestigious sports club. Our children were babies then and it was hard work. One day they offered a trip to France to whoever sold the most products over the next two years. I was part-time, but I sold twice as much as anyone else and won the trip. But when I returned from France, I realized that my commission was maxed and it wasn't possible to earn any more.

Getting Started in Real Estate

Since I obviously knew how to sell and was good with people, Joe suggested I try real estate. In May of 2007, I got my real estate license, just as the economy crashed.

No one trusted a young woman with no experience to sell or list their home. My wealthy clients at the spa trusted me with their skin, but not with their homes. It was costing me a lot of money to keep my desk in a real estate office. At one point we had $186 in the bank and a $280 utilities bill.

Meanwhile, the economy wasn't getting better, and people were starting to lose their homes. My natural question was, "If folks are losing their homes, who sells them?"

I Make My Big Move

I realized that banks needed agents to sell these repossessed homes. I started cold calling banks to get on their lists of preferred agents. Despite having no experience or market knowledge, I was determined to get in. We were in a new economy. Most agents back then had experienced only good markets. After months of cold calling and meeting with banks, I finally signed an agreement with one, which led to contracts with more banks.

What a crazy rollercoaster it was. I truly believe selling bank-owned homes is what really taught me to do this job right. I was constantly graded on my performance, just like in high school. Operating in a declining market, I had to price properties within 10 percent of their value six months prior to listing, or I lost points. If I couldn't convince the occupants to take a "cash for keys" check and move out, I lost points. If I didn't pick up the phone on the first ring or said the wrong thing when asset managers called and pretended to be buyers, guess what happened? If I received enough "demerits," my relationship with that bank was finished. We depended on them for our living and most other agents were going bankrupt in that great recession, so I really had to learn the industry and get my stuff in order.

The job was very emotional and I believe this prepared me for being a landlord in some ways. I had to meet with families and explain that their house no longer belonged to them. Many cried. Some had no idea where to go. Many had taken loans they had no hope to repay. Others were builders who had overextended themselves. Most left quietly. Two tried to kill me.

One packed barrels of kerosene in his garage and tried to blow up the house. Another flooded his house and placed wires in the water to electrocute anyone who came in.

Guess who was buying the bank-owned homes I listed? Investors! The real estate investment community was, and still remains, very tight lipped, but I came to know most of the top dogs in our area. We formed support groups to tackle common problems. We still call and consult with each other, and sometimes grab coffee together just to cry on each other's shoulders.

Now that I was seeing how real estate investors worked, I was more determined than ever to buy something. That's when I found that duplex in the snow. I had to borrow money from my father for the repairs, but I fixed it up and rented out both sides. Shortly afterwards, the area was redeveloped and became popular.

Enough of Analyze/Paralyze—Time to Buy

I started buying foreclosures at auctions. I was making money now, working with the banks, and that enabled me to buy a fourplex and then a triplex. They were in rough areas with lots of problems. One of my tenants was run over by another tenant's car. There was a drug overdose in one unit and the police were regular visitors.

From our experience with those buildings, I learned a lot about screening tenants and making repairs. When I finally stabilized the properties, I sold them. The economy was better now and I earned nice profits, which I immediately invested into a larger building.

I sold our duplex and bought a thirteen-unit apartment complex with the profits. When I researched it, people said the building was in a bad part of town. The police explained that it was a bad part of town due to *our building*. By the time I took possession, there were only four paying tenants out of thirteen units. The few remaining tenants were shocked when, one week after I took possession, a small army of workers showed up to fix things. I was determined to turn that building around. Three months later, I received a call from the town hall, thanking me for improving the neighborhood.

Lots of people were moving to that area. I'd love to think it was because I improved my building, but it was really because no one could afford to live near Seattle anymore. Rents increased and the property became very profitable.

Soon, I had money to buy more properties, but everything in the area was so overpriced. I knew that prices wouldn't rise forever, so I had to switch gears and focus on cash flow. My problem was that the numbers didn't make sense anymore.

Making Sense of Market Changes

I tried a few different things. I did flips and bought a few houses to hold. I began buying buildings without even showing them to Joe. The best properties didn't stay on the market long, so I had to make quick decisions. I remember closing on a home that my husband saw after I got the keys, and he hated it. Well, that was shocking to me, but I showed him that it still had cash flow. Two years later I sold that home and 1031 exchanged it to purchase a thirty-unit apartment complex with the proceeds. Did you catch that? I exchanged one home for a thirty-unit apartment complex. (I'll talk about how later.)

Our investments were making money, but I knew I could do better. That's when one of my investors told me about an out-of-state deal. Toyota was building a large factory and needed homes for executives arriving from Japan. The investor didn't have enough money to buy all the houses they needed, so he asked if I wanted to buy five homes. That night I came home and told Joe we were buying five homes out of state. *Not so fast*—this time he stopped me.

"If they're going to add all those jobs, we're buying apartment complexes, not homes," he said.

Sure enough, he was right. We bought more apartment complexes. Things were doing so well that we eventually sold everything we had in Washington state and moved it all to out-of-state apartments. The numbers were crazy! The home that Joe had hated was cash flowing $6,000 per year. The apartment complex we 1031 exchanged it to brought in $120,000 a year.

Looking Back

I began to work with real estate investors who wanted to replicate our success. I helped them avoid the pitfalls that we'd encountered earlier. Many of them have since retired, living off the rents from their buildings.

It's been quite a journey getting to where I am now. I find it funny that every so often I come across an agent, usually in commercial real estate, who insists that I have no experience. Of course, they have no idea how many units I own, how many hundreds of units I've sold, or the number of millionaires I've created.

Today I remember all the experiences that brought me to this point. I now lecture to rooms full of people in a language that was completely incomprehensible to me when I moved here at nineteen. Each of them earns more money than I ever would have dreamed of back then, but they seem to listen to me, perhaps because I've been in the trenches of real estate warfare.

As I read through my own story, I think that maybe this *is* a motivational book. If you're reading it, I assume you can speak English. You understand basic things like how to get bread and laundry detergent. You don't buy bad apples from the grocery store. You can absolutely do this. Really, the only thing preventing you from achieving success in real estate is your own inhibitions.

Let me show you how it's done.

Chapter 2
Decision Making

THE FIRST AND perhaps most important skill I help my clients with is decision making. In the country I came from, where our homes often lacked power or water, and gathering enough food was a daily challenge, I learned the importance of generating money.

Let's Learn How to Actually Make Money
In America, everyone is taught to study hard. If you do, you're likely to get good grades and go to a top college or university. There, if you study hard, a good company may hire you. The thinking goes that the harder you work, the more money you'll make. The more you make, the more you can spend.

Where I came from, getting a job wasn't too difficult, but the pay was insignificant. If you wanted something like a car or even a nice steak, you had to figure things out. You made deals with people. You determined what they needed and what you could offer. If you didn't do that, your life sucked.

Imagine - and this may not be far-fetched - that you want a house twice as large as your current home. To buy that house, you'll work extra hard at your job to get a promotion. How much more will you make after you receive it? If you're lucky, your salary will go up ten percent, or maybe even twenty percent. Will you be able to afford a home twice as large as your current one with twenty percent more money? Probably not. To buy that house, you're going to need to be more creative.

The Magical Money Tree

Imagine, for a moment, that you live in a fairy tale kingdom where you can plant money in the ground and trees grow that produce more money. When you receive your paycheck, you may therefore plant whatever you don't spend. The more money you bury in the ground, the more your money orchard will produce.

Anyone with half a brain would plant some of their money. In fact, there would be entire classes on how to cultivate your money trees to provide the most income. Someone would probably write a book about it. In such a kingdom, it would be obvious that the best way to wealth would be to propagate the money you earn and not push yourself to the breaking point to move up the corporate ladder and increase your salary. Now, here's the kicker. We already live in such a kingdom.

The major difference is that instead of just planting the money in the ground, you need to use it to buy something that grows the money. In this case, it's real estate. If you truly want to grow your wealth, you need to stop spending everything you earn and instead put time into allowing what you have earned to make you more. Just like in that fairy tale kingdom, you need to plant your money and learn how to make it bear fruit.

Now, don't come up with excuses about why you don't have enough money. If my parents could save enough to buy a house through washing dishes and sewing clothes, you can figure out how to save something. You don't need a lot. You also don't have to spend tens of thousands on courses teaching you how to save and invest money. Spending money on expensive courses enables those gurus and coaches to invest, not you.

How much money do you need? As much as you can gather. In our magical kingdom, if you plant a thousand dollars, you may make a hundred each year. If you plant a million, you may make a hundred thousand. The more money you plant, the more you make. There's no need to keep piling it up for that amazing tree. Start with what you have and build from there. However, money trees also work like fruit trees. If you don't know how to cultivate and care for them, they don't produce any fruit or your fruit will rot. This also applies to money. If you invest it poorly, you'll lose it.

This Is a Business

Later, I'll go into the specifics of how to buy and manage properties, but for now we'll focus on decision-making. This is often the stage when people make their biggest mistakes.

You have to remember that this is a business. You don't need to be mean, but you also don't have to be nice. Your goal is to make money. I've named this book *Nothing Held Back* for a reason. A lot of investors won't tell you this. If your goal is to feel better about yourself by changing your tenants' lives, it's not going to happen through real estate.

Many people have dreams of being the world's best landlord. They imagine perfect buildings with lovely people who look just like them, singing and dancing about how great their landlord is. They imagine buckets of money pouring in from the sky. Even when you're nice, many of your tenants won't like you. I'm not saying you need to be a wicked witch, but you have to recognize that this is a business.

I want to help you understand what this business is truly like and the decisions you'll have to make. If you're not prepared for what's about to come, you'll be eaten alive.

Chapter 2

My First Lesson

Early in my real estate investment career, an elderly man applied for a unit I was renting. He was a nice old man and his application looked fine. When I ran his credit, everything looked good, so I offered him the unit. He was very happy. Then he mentioned that he had forgotten to add that he had back surgery coming up, so his caregiver would live with him for two weeks afterwards. This again seemed reasonable, so I agreed.

Well, this so-called "nurse" turned out to be a crackhead girlfriend with an outstanding arrest warrant for drug dealing. She threw a wild party and someone overdosed and died in the parking lot. I received a call from a tenant at four in the morning with the news, though there was little I could do at the time. Luckily, the police were already there. They arrested his "nurse" and removed the deceased. Shortly after, the old man stopped paying his rent and I filed the eviction.

He had no money and nowhere to go. Because I didn't want him on the street, I did some research and called his two kids. Both lived in a nearby state. Both stated that their father was a lost cause and refused to house or help him in any way. He dragged it out until the court date, but since the lease clearly said he needed to pay rent and he wasn't doing that, they ruled in my favor.

The sheriff arrived to remove him from my apartment building and I watched this old man aimlessly walk down the street. My suspicions that he became homeless were confirmed several months later when an agency called and said they'd picked him up and were helping with his debts. They wanted to know how much he owed us, but I told them to forget about the money and help him instead.

What did I learn from this? I need to qualify *everyone* who lives in a unit even if it's for two weeks. Tenants will try to sneak others in, especially those who would be disqualified by a simple credit check. I also had to stop renting with my heart, but that lesson required another example before I learned it.

An Emotional Support Monster

One day, a church group called about one of my vacant units. They had a single mother who needed a place. She had several kids and had been through a lot. The church offered to pay whatever part of the rent she couldn't afford, so I was guaranteed payment. I met the woman and she seemed very nice. She was trying to turn her life around by taking classes at a community college so she could earn enough to support herself and her children. I felt this was a win-win, so, after running her credit, I gave her a chance.

Things turned sour immediately when she moved in. Once the lease was signed, she calmly stated that she had an "emotional support dog." It was a pit bull. I allowed pets in the building, but they had to be less than twenty pounds and there was a pet deposit. Because she had labeled it as "emotional support," I couldn't enforce either condition.

Soon after she moved in, her pit bull mauled another tenant's legal dog. She let her pit bull run around off leash and it terrorized the neighbors, but our state's laws prevented me from doing much.

Our other tenants were scared every time they went outside, but there was absolutely nothing I could do. The neighbors called the police, but because the animal was for "emotional support," they couldn't remove it. Eventually I started to lose tenants. Since she was paying her rent now without the church's help, I couldn't evict her. I'd love to say that I came up with some creative solution for the problem, but the truth is I didn't. I simply sold the building.

That was the end of accepting "feel good" tenants. I'm sure there are some decent people out there who are truly in unfortunate circumstances, but too many simply want to take advantage. They prey upon people who naively think they can help the world. After that, everyone had to qualify for themselves. I do continue to advise tenants who have paid for some time but are having temporary financial difficulties to consult with various charities for assistance, but I no longer take on project tenants.

These are the easy stories. In both cases, I failed to do something important. The next one, though, was more difficult.

A Tough Goodbye

This next tenant should have been a success story. She easily qualified for paying the rent. She was another single mother, rough around the edges, but she had a job and required no assistance. Every time I went to check on the building for some issue or repair, I stopped by to see her. She had a difficult past but was trying to turn a corner. She kept her unit very clean and was always quick to alert me to potential issues.

Unfortunately, she just couldn't escape her past. She started doing drugs and we saw each other less. She began to neglect her kids and one day social services took them away. I don't know the details that made them do this, nor do I want to know. She spent so much on drugs that she started to offer herself for money, but she spent that on drugs too. Eventually, she had no money to pay the rent.

It was painful, but I filed for eviction. Then one day, she just left. She sold everything she had in the apartment, then sold my washer and dryer, too. She broke into the unit a few times while it was vacant, but once I rented it again she never came back.

From a business viewpoint, I had done the right thing. Some people just can't fix their lives. As a landlord, that's not my problem. Still, it was difficult seeing such a good person destroy herself and her children.

Supplemental Income

This next story is more positive. This woman was another single mother (I know, I have a thing for them) and her application and credit checked out fine, so I rented to her. Like the woman in the previous story, she was always friendly and provided great information about what was happening in the building. One day, as part of a building maintenance inspection, I entered her unit. In the center of her bedroom was a stripper pole.

Clearly, this was supplemental income for her. I am not so naïve to think that stripping was her only profession. So what did I do? Absolutely nothing. She was a great tenant. She always paid in cash on time and never complained, and no one in the building complained about her. It was none of my business how she earned a living.

These last two cases illustrate that we should never get involved in our tenants' lives. We should also not hold them to our own standards. Certainly, if I had a daughter and found a stripper pole in her bedroom, the earth would shake. But these are simply business arrangements, nothing more. I provide shelter and tenants pay me for it. I truly don't get involved in my tenants' professions unless they're doing something that endangers others, such as drug dealing or child molestation. Even then, I let the police deal with the situation.

From these last several examples, I believe I've made it evident that you cannot get emotional over tenants. The same applies to properties.

Say Hello to My Little Lawsuit

Up until the last day, a particular property acquisition had been relatively normal. Sure, there had been negotiations over price and repairs, but they had been amicable. Our loan went through without issues and, on closing day, funds were wired from our bank to escrow. The property, however, didn't close.

The seller refused to close. He'd neglected to learn what "yield maintenance" meant on a loan, and the interest rates had fallen that day. Because his loan required him to pay the bank's losses due to a lower loan rate for the remainder of the term, that meant a very significant prepayment penalty on his part. Making matters worse for him, he was a syndicate (explained later, but in short a group of investors). He'd sold the property because he needed to dissolve his partnership and the hefty prepayment penalty meant his partners wouldn't get the proceeds he'd promised.

Complicating this on our end, we were on the last day for closing on a 1031 exchange. The seller had dragged his feet so long that we'd reached this point. It was a Friday, and if we didn't close that day, we'd owe several hundred thousand dollars in taxes. We needed this to close, and on our part, we had performed.

The seller wanted to delay several days to see if interest rates went up. I refused. Up to that point, I'd never sued anyone, nor had I been sued myself. My attitude had always been to resolve things far before litigation, but this time I ran it by my lawyer and made it absolutely clear to the seller that a lawsuit would proceed if he did not perform. Even escrow, which is supposed to be neutral, agreed that the seller would be at fault.

With five minutes until the recording office closed, the seller signed off and the transaction was complete. He'd known that I had both the desire and the legal means to make this far more painful financially than he would face from the prepayment penalty. Ultimately, he needed the sale to be complete so he could return whatever money he could to his partners.

Destroying Mental Blocks

I hope these stories have provided some of the realities of life in real estate. While some may scare you, we made money from every one of these buildings, even the one with the pit bull. I always say: "It's like getting paid to go to university without paying tuition." To put you in the right frame of mind to make money, the following are important mental blocks to escape.

First, you're not renting to people like yourself. Get over that. I don't know how many times I've rolled my eyes at my clients because they were looking for low-income housing with granite countertops and stainless-steel appliances. I've also had to tell my clients to stop calling their tenants. They're not your friends. Decisions involving them need to be what's best for the business.

Second, and this one's even more important, you need to think on your feet. Analyze/paralyze will absolutely ruin your chances of success. Can you decide whether to spend a million dollars on a property in an hour? Don't worry, I'll teach you how to do that, but you need to be mentally ready for it. You must get used to making decisions based on experience and the data immediately available to you. Sometimes those will be the wrong decisions, and you can't fret about that either. Instead, pick yourself up, dust yourself off, and figure things out.

So can you grow a thick skin and a cold, calculating business sense, and are you ready to make some decisions? Good. We're going to set you up for using these very soon, but first we need to focus on the absolutely most important aspect of real estate.

Chapter 3
Building Relationships

I'VE SEEN A lot of bad moves from real estate investors. However, absolutely the stupidest move I ever witnessed was an investor trying to lower an agent's commission. Imagine someone walking around with checks for $97,000. You ask the guy, "Why $97,000 instead of $100,000?" and he replies, "I keep $3,000 for myself." Are you seriously going to bargain him out of that $3,000?

Well, guess what he's going to do? Yup. He'll move on to the next person, and that's exactly what a commercial real estate agent, or any agent who focuses on investments, will do. Why? Because these agents are literally gold mines. They're *millionaire* makers. When a hot property comes their way, they decide which of their clients gets it.

Remember back in grade school when everyone who wanted a lollipop raised their hand, and the teacher was supposed to be fair? Well, this isn't fair. If you try to bargain that agent down, she is not only going to pass you by, she's going to label you as not serious. That's a death sentence in this business.

When an agent hands a property to one of her clients, that buyer needs to perform. What does "perform" mean? It means that if she brings you a property that *meets* your criteria, you put an offer on it, and when you say you'll buy it, you follow through. This is of vital importance to the agent because the seller's going to ask her to vouch for the buyers, and if you back out for a stupid reason, she has mud on her face.

Life in the Dog Pound

I hope I've reinforced that your agent is your investment lifeline. He or she will make you or break you.

This is a chapter on relationships, and the power dynamics vary with each professional you'll meet. I'll start by making your relationship with your agent very clear.

Imagine you're a small mangy dog in a room packed with hungry mutts. Occasionally, your real estate agent throws a bone into the crowd. You want that bone. You need that bone. You're therefore going to be the best dog possible, so the agent throws that bone your way, and when you get that bone, you're going to snarl and devour it.

Nevertheless, your odds of getting that bone aren't great. Most of the other dogs are bigger than you are. They're used to getting bones, and the agent likes those dogs more than you. A lot of big juicy bones with meat on them are going to be tossed into that room and you're never going to get a sniff.

But one day, the agent's going to have an ugly crusty bone that the big dogs don't care for, and she's going to throw it near you. You're going to take that bone, devour it, and say "Thank you."

Now that I've explained the imbalance of power between you and your agent, I'll step back a bit. Relationships are the key to real estate investments. Without them, nothing happens. You won't receive new properties to buy. There won't be any contractors to fix your buildings. No one will show your units or help you rent them. You'll make tax and legal mistakes. Your loan payments will be too high. Your life will be a living hell.

Building a Team

Before we get into the nitty-gritty of finding and maintaining properties, we need to discuss teamwork. Your team will make you or break you in this business. For the introverts among you, either brush up on your personal skills or do what my engineer husband did: Marry someone who has them.

In later chapters, I'll go into the specifics of working with individual team members. For now, though, I'll list who they are: real estate agents, property managers, general contractors, office managers, lenders, insurance agents, pest control, landscapers, subcontractors, lawyers, CPAs, and accountants, to name a few.

Those of you who want to invest out of state will need to create your team well before you even dream of moving on a property. You should fly out there and meet them. Personally, I make an appointment with an agent to discuss the area and see some properties. Most good agents, after I've begged them to work with me, showed them my credentials and history of performing, and hounded them for several months, will give me an hour or two of their time. I'll then fly out there and schedule meetings with property managers and contractors for every waking hour of the day during my visit. For any lunch or dinner appointments, I always pick up the tab. Sure, they'll make money from any work, but they're really the ones doing me a favor.

Constructing that initial team can be a daunting task, especially if you're investing out of state. A quality agent is a great start because agents worth their pay will have an army ready to work with you. Finding such an agent can be a challenge, so I'll discuss that first.

How Not to Buy a Property

Absolutely the worst way to find an agent for an investment is to use your cousin Theodore, your friend who just got her license, or a recommendation from a coworker who just bought a condo. First, you need someone with actual investing experience. Granted, there are good commercial agents out there who move hundreds or even thousands of units each year but don't own a single property themselves. However, if the agent isn't in that category, you need to make sure she owns significant investments herself. Owning a couple of condos isn't "significant," nor is a fourplex or two.

You need an agent who lives and breathes the investment world. These agents are a different breed from those who primarily sell single-family residences. First, they're not nice. They've dealt with endless jokers and been through far too many property wars to sit around and be fake. Their phones are about to ring from someone more important than you are, so they'll be straight and to the point.

Note that in terms of commercial versus residential agents, there's a blur. First, if you're looking at properties to flip, single-family homes, or multifamily up to and including fourplexes, you'll primarily deal with residential agents. Commercial agents will sell you these, but more often as part of a real estate package deal or because you also buy larger buildings with them. Properties with more than five units are typically handled by commercial agents, but not always. Both types of agents can list and sell each other's properties.

So, what's the difference between a residential and commercial agent? Typically it's more about specialization. There are many types of commercial agents as most concentrate on a particular type of building. For example, there are commercial agents who only work with breweries. Residential agents typically are focused on single-family homes, but there's nothing to prevent one from turning to large multifamily buildings.

Finding Real Estate Agents

Now that you understand the difference between types of agents, how do you select one? There are two primary ways that I've found to be successful. First, you can research to find who lists the properties you want in that area. If you're looking below five units, then this isn't going to help much because properties like these are covered by a vast array of agents in most decent-sized cities. Larger properties are typically hoarded by an elite group of agents. The commercial world is also very different from residential in that agents predominantly prefer to sell their own listings. That means you need the listing agent to write up your offer if you want to have a chance at winning that property. Are you thinking more like a mangy dog in the pound now?

The second method, and perhaps the most effective one for smaller properties, is to ask for a recommendation from your lender. Note that I'm being specific about the lender here because there are gotchas that pertain to most other team members. Lawyers who specialize in real estate will often refuse to recommend anyone. A good real estate-focused accountant might recommend someone, but you need a fair amount of real estate before it makes sense to hire that accountant, so it's a chicken-and-egg scenario. Similarly, most property managers want to know at least a specific property you're looking at before they'll spend much time with you. Lenders, though, are used to working with newbies.

I'll deal with finding a lender in the chapter on lenders, but a recommendation should also indicate that this agent and lender are used to working with each other. This is important because the last thing you want is for your top two teammates to hate each other.

How to Gauge if an Agent Is Knowledgeable about Investments

Once you have an agent on the phone, you'll still need to screen them. For a list of questions, find any book on residential real estate, go to the chapter on interviewing agents, and make sure to never ask any of those questions. Really, you should just ask how long the agent has been doing this, how much inventory they own themselves, and roughly how many units they move a year. Note that if you selected your agent based on listings, then the last question is irrelevant.

In truth, an initial discussion with your potential agent shouldn't even be an interview. She should ask you how much you have to "play with" and what you're looking for. If you can't answer those questions quickly, many agents will politely move to end the call because you're obviously a jokester. In your case, that would also mean you didn't finish this book before calling them.

The agent should then go through some properties that she knows fit your criteria. You should say yes to a few, which just means she'll send you the info. Note that you most often won't see properties before you place an offer on them. The exception is when an out-of-state agent may take the time to show you one or two example properties so you can evaluate the typical inventory in the area.

What I'm really saying, in terms of "interviewing" an agent, is that a proper investments agent will simply act professional and to the point. A knowledgeable agent will already know what's available in the area and can summarize it off the top of her head. If this is a hot market, she may list some previous sales that would have met your criteria. A great agent will also emphasize setting up your team. She'll ensure you have the right lender and, if you don't have a team set up to move on a property, she'll provide recommendations to get you started.

Why Cheap People Lose

Finally, perhaps the second foolish request a new buyer can make, after suggesting an agent reduce their commission, is asking the agent to send hot deals your way. I'm sure you're familiar with the adage "There's no such thing as a stupid question." I can assure you, in my profession, there is. Why is this a red flag?

This agent already has a list of buyers she trusts. They'll get those amazing deals, not you. Even if you come into her office with a bag stuffed with millions of dollars and a willingness to purchase anything she offers you, you're not going to get those deals. No. You're going to get that overpriced complex with environmental issues that every sane buyer has already passed on, but you're too much of a newbie to turn down. Nothing you say is going to get you those "hot" deals. That will depend on what you *do*. Earn her trust by acting and performing on buildings that meet your criteria, and you'll move up her list.

Rest assured, though, that she does want to sell you something. You've told her what you want and if that exists, and no one more important than you wants it, then she'll send it to you.

It's best to skip the complaining and the bargaining. Make clear to agents how much money you have to play with and what your parameters are. If you don't know your parameters, I cannot over-emphasize the benefit of continuing to read this book. I'll tell you everything I know about this, but I can't do my job if you keep putting down your book to call agents.

Now you may think I have this all easy since I'm an agent myself. While it's true that I am an agent, I'm only licensed in Washington state. When I buy in any other state, which I do often, I need an agent myself. In those cases, I am entitled to a referral fee that I *never* ask for and am in the exact same boat as all other buyers. Why don't I ask for a referral fee? I don't want that agent to worry about paying me $10,000 and therefore not send a deal my way that I could potentially make millions on.

Keeping Your Team Happy

Now we'll move ahead to when you have your dream team in place. Yes, I'm allowed to skip around. Your team is in place and you have your first property or properties. As I mentioned, the people on your team are the difference between your success and retirement, and your failure and bankruptcy. Knowing that, do you micromanage and berate them? No. That would be a foolish thing to do, although many who fail do just that.

You need to constantly keep your team happy. How do you do that? You can start by making sure to show your appreciation. Take them out to lunch periodically. Personally, I fly out to my properties at least once every three to six months and take my property manager, her directs, and some of our contractors out to lunch. We chat about pretty much everything except politics. Note: You should *never* discuss politics with your team. There's a high likelihood that you're on opposite sides of the political spectrum and remember that this is just business. You should also only friend your real estate team on social media if you're not political there. Even if you aren't, it's often best not to get into each other's personal lives.

There's one thing that's not political, and that's money. Everyone likes it. Do send your team members gift cards to show your appreciation, especially when they go above and beyond. If a team member is stressed after dealing with some difficult tenants but does a great job in handling them, get her a gift card to her favorite spa. Call to congratulate her on her amazing work, but show it too.

There's also a hidden motivation behind all this praise. When something goes wrong at one of your properties, and it will, you'll want them to think of you first. Contrary to what you might imagine, contractors and other professionals don't sit around all day waiting for your call. They have many other properties to see to, but when you really need them, they'll remember who scratched their back last.

What to Do When People Upset You

No discussion about building a team is complete without mentioning what you should do when a member of that team inevitably upsets you. This will happen, and you're going to need to handle it. Let's discuss the possible ways they can upset you.

The most obvious way to upset you involves money. Now some may recommend that you obtain a quote in writing along with an itemized list of what will be done before any work is started. That's great advice when you're redoing *your* kitchen, but not-so-great advice when investing in property. While I'll discuss this in more depth in the chapter on building maintenance, here's the short version: If someone gives you a high bid, you don't work with them. It's that easy. There's no back-and-forth bargaining. You just thank them for their time and move on. If a contractor who used to be cheap raises his rates too high, you find a new one. There's nothing personal about this. It's business!

The next way people can upset you is by doing a lousy job. Absolutely the worst thing you can do in this case is lose your temper. Your enemies will find you in this industry so there's no need for you to manufacture them yourself. Always be nice and ask questions. Instead of "You (*(# moron! How in the *#(#& could you drywall the outlet for the refrigerator!?" you should say "Hmmm… I'm just wondering. We're going to put a refrigerator here, but we seem to be lacking an outlet. What can we do about that?" If the contractor continues to mess up, then stop giving him business and find someone new.

I cannot stress enough that you should never, ever lose your temper or burn your bridges. One day you're going to have a problem that needs to be fixed immediately, and your top person for the job will be on vacation in Kathmandu. What are you going to do? Yes, you'll pick up the phone and call that guy who did a horrible job because you're desperate. You're going to pretend that the last time he worked for you was yesterday, and you're going to praise and thank him if he agrees to help.

For an illustrative example, one day my insurance provider called to inform me they'd cancelled my policy. I was furious. Why!? It was nothing personal, but that company no longer serviced my area. Fine. I asked my broker to find another agency, but he now had nothing in the area. Perturbed, I called other brokers until I found a policy that worked and moved to that company. A year later, the new company doubled my rate! Prices were going up everywhere, and they decided to take advantage of the opportunity.

What was I going to do? I called back my original insurance agent, pretended we'd talked just yesterday, and asked if he had anything. Sure enough, within the last year he'd made new partnerships and I was able to move my insurance to a new company for only a slight premium increase. Good thing I didn't burn that bridge!

Perhaps the worst way someone can make you angry is intentionally. Recently, I wanted to buy an apartment building. I knew the owner and had previously spoken to him about purchasing his building. One day he called to ask if I still wanted to buy it. I did, so I called my agent to write the offer. I had to use an agent because this was out of state, and I was a good dog and hoped it would lead to better bones.

I expected to get the property, but instead, my call alerted the agent to a bone for one of his bigger clients, and he ensured that his other buyer got the property even though we offered the same amount. I was not happy about this.

I'm sure some of you would have threatened the agent with lawsuits, and screamed and cried and been no better from the ordeal. But while I *did* voice my displeasure, I never yelled, nor did I stop working with this agent. This discussion could have been very heated, but it was instead cordial. Eventually things worked out for the best, as I've now learned that the building had undisclosed problems.

The agent in this case knew I would be upset but did it anyway. And guess what? That's just part of this business. If you can't handle situations like these maturely, then you don't belong here. In business, sometimes people work for you and sometimes they're against you. It's always changing. It's just business.

Chapter 4
Networking

HAVE YOU EVER watched one of those movies where the hero joins a super-secret group of people who teach him or her how to do super-secret stuff? What the movie didn't show was that the hero first tried to join a real estate investor network but was rejected.

Yes, investors are notoriously tight lipped. There are numerous reasons for it, but the desire to limit competition isn't high among them. It's because we know most people out there are going to mess up. They're going to get involved in that hopeless project and pour their hearts, souls, and money into it. Then they'll be forced to sell at a heavy discount and we'll either buy it then or after the bank repossesses it.

Why Seasoned Investors Are Skittish

What we're afraid of is newbies. That's really it. We're tired of being asked the same questions over and over, so we stick to people who don't ask them—other investors with similar experience to ours. We're investors, not babysitters. We have enough problems to deal with of our own without taking on someone else's.

While the prospect of networking with investors may seem daunting, that doesn't mean you can't network with people who will teach you something. Learning more about the field is a great first step to breaking into this business. In addition to reading this book, read others concerning tax and legal concepts. Create your "real estate model," which I'll cover later. Essentially, get all the basic questions out of the way before focusing on meeting other investors.

How to Meet Other Investors

One option is to meet with other new investors or with those who own fewer than ten units and are thus also green in the field. You'll all face similar problems, so you'll certainly learn things. If you search around a bit, you'll find groups that discuss investing. These meetings can provide valuable information, but keep in mind that there might be more falsehoods than facts floating around. Remember that every one of the group members is struggling, too, and anyone with under ten units who states he knows what he's doing doesn't know what he's doing.

A less successful approach is to approach bigger investors and try to pick their brains. Since I'm an agent who also invests, I'm often approached. I'll share with you what has worked and what hasn't.

Candidate A bombarded me with questions for a while. I knew for a fact he'd already bought with a different agent. As is typically the case, that agent had no clue about investments but did have her real estate license, so she sold him a small multifamily property that made little financial sense, then left him to wallow in the dust. He called me for advice, but what motivation did I have to babysit him?

Candidate B initially touched base with me with a few questions. Our discussion was short and his questions were direct. Sometime later, he contacted me with a property. It was too much for him to take on, but he thought I'd either want it or know someone who did. The property was intriguing, so I sent it to one of my clients, who purchased it.

Guess which candidate I'm going to call when I see a small property with great numbers? That's right. Candidate B is on my "good list" now. And even when I don't have something that works for him, I'll gladly share information.

Whatever you do, please don't go knocking on doors and become a wholesaler. There are a distinct set of people who attempt to make a living finding suckers who don't know the value of their properties. Wholesalers lock their marks into a low price and then shop the properties to investors. The idea is to make a profit in the transaction, during which both parties see you as the scum of the earth. Most investors steer clear of known wholesalers at social engagements. Cheating others out of what they're due is not a way to endear yourself to people.

There are also lurkers, who sit around the offices listening to other agents' deals, then relay that information to other offices' agents in exchange for a referral fee. Instead of partaking in either activity, you should just get to know people.

One tactic that numerous books recommend but that I find rarely works in practice is the old "Can I borrow thirty minutes of your time?" approach. Please understand, you can't expect me to give you every secret I know over the five-dollar coffee you just bought me. Don't take it personally, but that puts me in the awkward position of refusing.

However, you *can* ask if they teach any classes or have a business social media presence. I'm always happy to provide that information and I'm sure most other investors are too. If they don't participate in either of these, ask if they know of any. You may be surprised.

Hosted classes are a good way to learn. Many agents and industry professionals offer them. Some are better than others. Look for those that bring guest speakers on important real estate issues. Steer away from those that appear only intended to advertise themselves. You should also look for classes on social media, as some are live streamed. If you can, try to attend in person because you can usually chat directly with industry professionals who may have set aside time for random questions.

Networking in Your Neighborhood

Once you buy a property, a tremendous source of information is the other property owners in your area. Find out who owns the adjacent buildings and give them a call. It can be for as simple a reason as to introduce yourself. If you don't say something foolish like lamenting the dilapidated state of their building or asking their tenants to stop throwing beer cans on your lawn, they'll sometimes share some juicy news with you. This is the primary way I learn that properties are for sale off market.

Behind one of my buildings is a much larger complex. During a chat with the owner, I learned he wanted to sell it. In this case, I simply didn't have the funds, so I called my agent and let him know. He listed and sold the property. How much did I make from that transaction? Absolutely nothing! But shortly after that, my agent passed me a building I *was* interested in, and today it's a very, very profitable star in my portfolio.

Do you see the pattern? During networking, it's not about money. When you try to profit off someone else's transaction by asking for a fee, you're going to earn their ire. They'll go around you at the next opportunity. If you really want to get ahead, then it's more "You scratch my back and I'll scratch yours."

Perhaps my biggest deal so far came to me via one of my clients. I'd sold him several properties and gotten him started in his career. He found a deal with executive housing out of state that was too big for him to finish, so he invited me. I wound up not biting on that deal, but I did purchase several apartment buildings nearby. In that case, a tip from a fellow investor introduced me to an extremely profitable area.

In my experience, it pays to meet with other investors whenever you can. Sometimes a single statement can trigger a light bulb in your head. Lunch is often the easiest opportunity, but make sure to not talk too much. Ask your questions, then shut up - and I mean zip it - and listen.

The next piece of advice you may find shocking. I'm liberal in terms of with whom I meet. What does this mean? There's one investor who my husband loathes. This investor has rather unethical business practices, to say the least. He used to be my client, and I showed him the ropes and my system and guided him through his first several properties. Of course, he must have had other mentors since I didn't teach him the practices he executes now. Every time I chat with him, Joe asks me why.

The simple reason is I often learn useful market information. My former client still buys and sells properties, though without my representation. It's useful to know where he has a difficult time renting and his solutions to regular building maintenance problems. He never receives anything interesting that comes my way, but I do learn things from our meetings.

My recommendation is always to meet with all sorts of people in your investment community, even those you may find repulsive. Just avoid getting into actual transactions with them, and I guarantee you'll benefit.

For those who do increase your bottom line, make sure to thank them properly. Personally, I take several of my top clients out to nice dinners or events every year. Before you spend that money, verify that it's somewhere they'd want to go. For example, don't buy seats for a baseball game only to discover your clients don't like the sport.

Making Yourself Findable

I'll end this chapter by discussing whether you should let others find *you*. This advice is certainly controversial, since it's counterintuitive if your goal is to abstract your property ownership through trusts. Simply put: Should you expose your contact information in county records?

A lot of people will tell you no, because they don't want their tenants to find them. More importantly, some investors obfuscate ownership through trusts in states like Nevada and Delaware to make it more difficult for lawyers to sue them personally. Entire books are written about this.

However, I offer one major reason to say yes: It allows interesting people to find you. Real estate firms pick up my information and call me, and that's exactly what I want. Why? Because they list other properties. They may know about other buildings coming up for sale. While I have no plans to let them sell mine, they may have something interesting available. They may also have some good gossip about properties in my area. Therefore, I don't mind chatting with them.

If you want to network, at times you need to let the network come to you. It's true that exposing your personal information will make it easier for lawsuits to reach you, but in my experience, lawyers are pretty good at finding the liable parties when it matters.

Chapter 5

Math Stuff

THIS CHAPTER MAY be the most important one in the entire book. Here, I'll tell you how I determine mathematically whether a property makes sense. Yes, this chapter contains math. I know. I hate it too; in fact, I failed math in high school. That's why I married a guy who likes it.

Real estate investing, and probably all investing, is a numbers game. What you're going to do is take a building (usually) filled with living, breathing people, and generate a few numbers. You'll then look at those numbers. If you like them, you'll buy the building.

Your Math Teacher Wouldn't Like Real Estate Math

Before I explain those numbers, there's an extremely important caveat that I must discuss. Do you remember back in math class when your teacher would put a problem up on the board and you'd have to solve it? You either got it right, or (in my case) got it wrong. Now imagine that right after your teacher said you're wrong, you stood up and said, "Well, that's how I calculated it and there's nothing you can do about it."

In real estate investing, that's exactly how numbers work. For this reason, engineers tend to do poorly in this field. They just can't comprehend how someone can take a sheet full of numbers and come up with different answers. But it's true. Everyone has different ways of calculating. Of course, some methods make you money and some drain it away. Still, there's a generally agreed upon understanding in the industry that your numbers are your numbers, and you're only expected to act when your numbers tell you to.

Here's an even cooler aspect about real estate math. Do you remember back to things like geometry and calculus? Imagine you stood up in class and said, "Teacher, this is irrelevant to my needs, so I'm just going to play on my phone for the next few weeks." Again, your math teacher would have had a dim view of this statement.

Nevertheless, real estate math is full of useless stuff. This terminology is the number one way some individuals pretend to know more than others. You'll hear all sorts of terms during real estate podcasts, and their primary function is to make the speaker sound smart. In truth, there aren't too many terms that you really need to know. I'll discuss the important ones in this chapter. The rest I'll ignore.

Most of the terms I'm not listing here are easily discoverable through Google, and my advice, when a podcast or video starts rattling them off, is to switch to something else. In school, did you ever insert long words you didn't really know into a paper just to sound more intelligent? Yes? This is the same thing.

Before I get into math, I need to discuss numbers. Using the wrong numbers is easily the top mistake I've seen made by people evaluating properties. Most investors know the basic formulas, but if you put the wrong numbers in, you get the wrong numbers out! Remember that even though there's no one "right" number, you're staking hundreds of thousands, or even millions of dollars on them. Would you trust a random number generator to tell you whether an apartment complex was worth buying? After I explain the math, I'll discuss how to choose the right numbers.

Do you have your pen and paper ready? Good. Put them away and open up Notepad or Excel. Seriously, stop using so much paper, we're trying to save the earth. Of course, don't let me bully you into which program to use. Personally, I use Excel most often, but I've also spent millions on a building evaluated with Notepad and iPhone calculator.

Term	When do you Care?	How Important is it?	Meaning
ROI	Buying	The most important	How much you will earn per year from your initial investment
Cap Rate	Buying	Marketing term that can be ignored	How much you will earn per year if you pay all cash
eROI	Selling	Very	By how much will you increase your earnings if you sell now and buy something else
Every other term	Never	Not at all	Makes the speaker sound smarter than you

Return on Investment (ROI)

The most crucial number for me when evaluating a property is Return on Investment, or ROI. What this tells me is: For each $100 that I invest up front into this property, how much will I receive each year? If you haven't noticed yet, I don't really go by how much the building will increase in value. Why? Because I don't know that.

Okay. I actually *do* know that. I've been pretty good at predicting the market, but I still buy based on ROI. I'm looking at yearly income and not at flips. Since I have a limited amount of cash on hand to buy properties, I want to maximize my income by purchasing the properties with the highest ROI. Some use the term "cash-on-cash," which is basically the same thing.

But in fact, there are two ROIs to be considered. The first ROI is the numbers the building is currently generating. If you buy the building and run it exactly as the sellers do today, how much will you earn from the cash put down? This is an extremely useful number that everyone except for lenders ignores.

The number most go by is called "pro forma ROI." Pro forma is what happens when a magical fairy spreads her pixie dust and all the rents come up to market value and the tenants start erecting statues in honor of their landlord. To put it another way, pro forma numbers are what the building would have earned were the seller running it correctly, with market rents and reasonable expenses.

The trick is, and this is really a revolutionary concept, when you buy the building, you *should* run it correctly! One time we backed out of a complex and another buyer picked it up. A year later they tried to sell it to us. They hadn't raised rents at all but had increased their pro forma numbers. We stayed with our earlier decision.

So now that you understand what we're calculating, it's time for the how.

$$ROI = \frac{yearly\ profit}{initial\ investment}$$

That's not so difficult. If you invest $100 and earn $21 per year, then:

$$ROI = \frac{21}{100} = .21 = 21\%$$

The Initial Investment

Now let's drill in on these numbers. First, what is the initial investment? This is always your down payment on the property and may sometimes include initial repairs. You'll need to speak with your lender to determine the down payment because it will vary by deal. How much a bank lends you will depend on the property's cash flow and on your investment experience. Yes. That means the bank will calculate their own numbers on the property. Still, you should be able to receive a ballpark figure for the required down payment ahead of time from your lender. At the time of writing this book, down payments of 25 percent or 30 percent are typical. Therefore, if the property costs $100,000 and your down payment is 25 percent:

$$Initial\ investment = \$100{,}000 \times .25 = \$25{,}000$$

Sometimes you may want to include your initial repairs in your initial investment. This is necessary when the building will only be habitable with some work. Other times, you may prefer to do repairs as funds are available. Now I'll discuss how to calculate yearly profit.

$$Yearly\ profit = (monthly\ income - monthly\ debits) \times 12$$

Calculating Rents

For each month, you're going to calculate your profits and expenses. Let's show this. Monthly income is usually comprised of one thing: rents. You need to calculate how much all the units in the building bring in. How do you know that? You ask the seller. For current numbers, the rents will be exactly what the seller reports, which you can verify with bank statements during the later due diligence period. For pro forma numbers, you should ask your agent but also verify for yourself that they're possible.

To verify pro forma rents, your best bet is to check local listings for apartments in buildings of similar age and size. If you already have a property manager, you can also consult her.

Be aware that many sellers will play with numbers a bit by declaring "loss to lease." For example, you may see on a fourplex that the rent is $1,000 per unit, then a monthly loss to lease of

$900. That means the units *should* rent for $1,000 per the seller-assessed market conditions, but they' are actually receiving $775 ($900 divided by four units is a $225 discount per unit, and thus they rent for $1000 - $225 or $775). Therefore, what the seller is *really* saying is the rents are $775. The next time someone asks you for twenty dollars, give him five and explain the other fifteen were lost to lease. These types of Mickey Mouse numbers are often used to generate a higher Cap rate, which I'll explain later.

Other numbers that you may include in profits are late fees and laundry income. Personally, I stick to rents. Other incomes are just not significant or consistent enough to change ROI. One potential complication may involve billing of utilities. In multifamily buildings without separate meters, some sellers choose to bill tenants for those utilities. Each seller does things differently, but the most typical arrangement is to either divide the actual costs evenly between tenants, or charge a precalculated flat fee amount. I prefer the latter, and when I calculate the ROI, I include these utility charges in the rent, then count the actual utility costs in the expenses.

Calculating Expenses

Calculating the monthly debits is a bit trickier and this is where everyone has a different approach. The following are some typical line items you'll find in the seller's report.

>**Advertising** – I never include this myself in expenses because there are too many free venues to advertise my units.
>
>**Appliances** – Yes, these break, but I include them under repairs.
>
>**Cleaning and Maintenance** – These costs are necessary unless you want your building to look like a dump. I usually lower someone's rent in the building in exchange for cleaning things up, but on large buildings this will be an expense. It's best to consult with your property manager on what the expectations

are. In the largest buildings you may have paid staff responsible for this.

Electricity – This is the utility most often paid through separate meters by the tenants, but that isn't always the case. The building may also have common areas and lighting that require electricity. If the numbers seem high, bring it up with the seller. I'll usually take whatever number the seller provides, and when I take possession of a property, I'll reduce costs by putting sensors in hallways, replacing older lightbulbs with LEDs, and turning off the lights in vacant units.

General Maintenance – This is proactive maintenance done to avoid repairs. The issue with calculating it in ROI is it varies widely from month to month. While it's possible to take an average over the year, even that can vary. For example, pressure washing the exteriors is only necessary every several years but can skew one particular year. My recommendation is to either fit this into a per-unit-per-month repair estimate or not include it. See below for my reasoning on why not to include it.

The one exception here is that properties over one hundred units will typically have an on-site maintenance person. This *is* a regular expense you can count on, and the salaries of any *repair* staff, need to be included in the ROI. This figure, however, does not include management, who I calculate separately.

Insurance – For estimation purposes, you can use numbers the seller provided. However, you should have a relationship already with an insurance professional, so ask him what the rough estimates per unit are in the area. If the seller's insurance numbers differ from those estimates, send the information you have to your agent for a rough quote. Be aware that you may have a very different rate from what the seller currently pays. The actual rate may be higher or lower as insurance companies' rates vary considerably. Note that we do require all renters to obtain renters' insurance.

Landscaping – I always include this, but I verify that the costs are in line with what I expect. Research what the going rates are for landscaping in the area. If this property has exorbitant fees, investigate why. Does it have an excessive amount of land or a lot of shrubbery? I've seen a few properties that pay too much for gardening services and have at times decided that I would fire the current landscaper and hire a cheaper one.

Legal – This is most often eviction fees, but there can be other legal expenses. I generally don't include this in the pro forma ROI because my goal is to not evict anyone. Of course, it's typical to evict a lot of people when taking over a building, but remember these are pro forma numbers. Eventually evictions sputter out when the building is stabilized. You'll never completely avoid evictions in larger buildings, but they should be infrequent enough to not significantly change your bottom line.

Management Fees – For some properties you'll see several expense categories here, and no other item causes as much anguish, because it's the easiest line item for the property manager to abuse. I *never* keep the current property management on after purchasing a property, though I don't tell them that up front. I have my own management team, with whom I have a strong working relationship and trust.

Too often I've seen very odd numbers under management fees, and it doesn't take a genius to suggest some fraud is happening. While this fraud doesn't concern *me*, because I'm going to let go of the current management, it can cause problems during financing. The lender will look at current numbers and if management fees prevent those numbers from looking attractive, I may not get the loan.

At times, crazy management fees or ridiculous line-item expenses may result in numbers that can threaten your ability to receive a loan, even if your pro-forma numbers are awesome. What do you do if this happens? In truth, this is why experience matters in real estate. You're going to need to convince the bank that the current numbers are due to mismanagement and that your pro-forma numbers are achievable. You'll accomplish this by showing them that you've succeeded with similar properties in the past.

In terms of calculating ROI, I ignore whatever numbers the seller includes here for management fees. Instead, I use the fees my own property manager charges. If you're self-managing your properties (more about that in Chapter 13), you can calculate management costs as zero.

> **Pest Control** – This is a fact of life in many southern state properties, and unlike maintenance and repairs, it has a consistent charge. Most pest professionals charge a monthly rate per unit, so this should be in the ROI.
>
> **Repairs** – Things break down, sometimes intentionally. There's no escaping that. This will vary by area. Consult with your property manager when estimating monthly repair costs. Remember that one appliance or major repair could amortize to over $100 per month for that unit in one year. There are two strategies here. Either include an estimated per-unit-per-month repair cost, or don't include it at all. See below for my reasoning on why not to include it.
>
> **Sewer** – This is often included with water, but not always. When included with water, it may be separately metered and paid by the tenants, but if not, it's often your responsibility. If this is an expense and looks high, check your city's sewer rates, which are often available online. Some cities have dramatically different rates from others, so don't assume the rates will be the same in a neighboring town.

Supplies – I lump these under repairs.

Taxes – Property taxes are public information but should be provided by the seller. In some states, taxes are reassessed after a building records, so factor in the estimated new taxes if the building is in one of those states. Otherwise, you can assume that the current numbers will remain roughly the same for the next year. When putting together a multi-year ROI (necessary for many loans), increase the tax estimate by a percentage each year.

Trash – This is an expense on almost every property. For small- to medium-sized buildings, make sure the trash containers are sufficient for the tenants. I've seen sellers skimp here and the result shows in the condition of the grounds. In some locations, this expense is combined with sewer.

Water – This is the most common utility cost, and the most wasted resource. In my experience, tenants have absolutely no care for how much water they consume unless the building units are separately metered and the tenants are responsible for paying for it. Always seek to replace shower heads and toilets with newer water efficient models. This is typically done as units are renovated, so it will take some time for the differences to show.

Note that different cities may have vastly different rates for water. If the number seems high, look up the city's rates online and calculate roughly how much water the building is using per unit. While the water costs may vary across locales, the usage should remain similar. Excessively high costs are therefore a sure sign that there are leaks. I'll often bring up any discrepancy with the seller before I'll recalculate the rates at a typical usage, with the assumption that I'll fix the leaks in the pro forma.

I have a bit of an unorthodox approach towards repairs. They're notoriously difficult to predict, and even a per-unit-per-month estimate is unlikely to be accurate. They also vary widely during the life of a property. Typically, when we take possession, we refinish many of the units and sweep through the property making repairs. This leads to a high initial cost, but much lower repair costs over the next three to five years. Therefore I just don't include them in the ROI.

Does this mean I foolishly believe there will be no repairs? Of course not. I simply adjust my target ROI upwards with the idea that, whatever the repair costs, the high ROI will compensate for them. This also makes it easier for me to compare property cash flows because the number of repairs will differ by building, and what I really want to know is how much income these buildings will generate when they are stable.

Note that I tend to take a more free-wheeling approach to numbers. Since it's nearly impossible to predict line-item expenses for every little thing, I work with the data the seller gives me, my own experience, and my property manager and contractor to calculate ballpark figures and use those. You're never going to have *exact* numbers. Even when you own the building and *can* calculate exact numbers, they'll vary each month.

So there you have it. All your expenses! Well, not quite. You're still missing one huge expense: Your mortgage. This will of course vary by how much you borrow, the interest rate, and whether you have an interest-only loan. To obtain these figures, ask your lender. Each calculation will be dependent on the property and the loan product.

An Excel Tip

This next piece is intended only to save some time for those of you who use Excel. The PMT macro enables you to calculate mortgage payments. When evaluating properties, I (mainly my husband) create a spreadsheet that enables me to play with numbers and understand how things like rents, loan term, interest rate, and sales price affect the ROI. The PMT macro removes what's otherwise the most complicated calculation. If I have my interest rate in field O14 (say 4.6 percent), my term in field O15 (say 30), and the loan amount in field D25, I can calculate the mortgage payment through.

$$= PMT(O14/12, O15 * 12, -D25)$$

Note that the number 12 is for the months in the year. To calculate interest only, the formula is much simpler.

$$=(O14/12)*D25$$

An Illustrated Example

You now have everything you need to calculate the ROI. To illustrate this, I'll use an actual property that we chose not to buy. This building had the following arrangement of units along with their average current rents. Here, BR stands for "bedroom" and BA stands for "bath." Some units are repeated because this property consisted of several complexes.

Unit Type	Quantity	Current Rent
1BR 1BA	80	634
1BR 1BA	12	636
1BR 1BA	4	894
2BR 1.5BA	14	771
2BR 1.5BA	28	707
2BR 1.5BA	32	761

Let's calculate the pro forma and yearly rents. Hold on while I call my property manager and… got it! Here's what we have:

Unit Type	Quantity	Current Rent	Pro Forma Rent	Current Monthly	Pro Forma Monthly	Current Yearly	Pro Forma Yearly
1BR 1BA	80	634	699	$50,720	$55,920	$608,640	$671,040
1BR 1BA	12	636	710	$7,632	$8,520	$91,584	$102,240
1BR 1BA	4	894	900S	$3,576	$3,600	$42,912	$43,200
2BR 1.5BA	14	771	900	$10,794	$12,600	$129,528	$151,200
2BR 1.5BA	28	707	900	$19,796	$25,200	$237,552	$302,400
2BR 1.5BA	32	761	900	$24,352	$28,800	$292,224	$345,600
3BR 1.5BA	4	716	950	$2,864	$3,800	$34,368	$45,600
Total	174			$119,734	$138,440	$1,436,808	$1,661,280

These calculations should be simple to follow. I'm just multiplying the number of units by the rent to obtain the monthly rent. Then I multiply the monthly rent by twelve to get the yearly rent. The important numbers here are $1,436,808, which is what we're currently collecting per year in rents, and $1,661,280, which is what we'll collect pro forma. Now let's calculate our annual expenses.

Chapter 5

	Current	Pro Forma
Management	$143,681	$166,128
Utilities	$44,755	$44,755
Exterminator	$7,100	$7,100
Insurance	$70,370	$70,370
Taxes	$79,260	$79,260
Maintenance	$94,445	$94,445
Garbage	$15,225	$15,225
Grounds	$28,950	$28,950
Total	$483,786	$506,233

Since our property manager charges a percentage, the management costs will vary by how much is collected in rents. For maintenance, I included the costs of keeping staff on site. The grounds expense included landscaping. Each of these is a yearly expense.

Let's say we paid $12,000,000 for the property. The interest rate is 4.6 percent for 30 years and we must put 25 percent down. What would our ROI be?

Our down payment will be

$$down\ payment = .25 \times \$12{,}000{,}000 = \$3{,}000{,}000$$

Our loan amount will be

$$loan\ amount = \$12{,}000{,}000 - \$3{,}000{,}000 = \$9{,}000{,}000$$

Our mortgage payment, using an online calculator or Excel, will be $46,138.

Therefore, the current ROI will be

$$current\ ROI = \frac{1{,}436{,}808 - 483{,}786 - (12 \times 46{,}138)}{3{,}000{,}000} = \frac{399{,}366}{3{,}000{,}000} = 13.3\%$$

We took the current amount we collect in rents, deducted our expenses, then deducted what we pay for the mortgage each year, and then divided by the amount we put down. Now let's calculate the pro forma ROI.

$$pro\ forma\ ROI = \frac{1{,}661{,}280 - 506{,}233 - (12 \times 46{,}138)}{3{,}000{,}000} = \frac{601{,}391}{3{,}000{,}000} = 20\%$$

The pro forma ROI should of course always be greater than the current ROI. If not, you need to fire the magical fairies.

It's worth noting that at the time I'm writing this, inflation is very high and property costs are soaring, so perhaps this will be the price of a medium-sized condo in a bad neighborhood by the time you read this. A point I'd like to make while using a property that today is considered expensive is that big buildings are evaluated exactly like small buildings. The numbers are calculated the same way, regardless of the size.

Cap Rate and Why It's Stupid

Now that I've explained ROI, I need to discuss the next most used number, which is the Cap (short for 'capitalization') rate. This number is heavily used in pricing properties but is mostly useless in evaluating them. The Cap rate basically says, "If I pay $100 for a building, how much will I make every year?" The major difference between it and ROI is Cap rate does not include loan expenses. It assumes you pay cash for the building.

The formula to calculate it is

$$Cap = \frac{profits - debits}{purchase\ price}$$

The important thing in the dividend (top part of the equation) is the mortgage *is not* factored at all. You simply sum up your rents, subtract your expenses, and divide by the purchase price of the property. Let's calculate the Cap for the building above.

$$Cap = \frac{1{,}436{,}808 - 483{,}786}{12{,}000{,}000} = 7.9$$

Note that this isn't the actual Cap listed for the property because we didn't include repairs. The true Cap rate will factor in all expenses from either the last year or the average over the previous three years.

The common purpose for the Cap rate is in pricing. Reversing the formula above:

$$list\ price = \frac{profit}{Cap}$$

Therefore, if the Cap rate is 5 percent and the property makes $100,000 per year after expenses but before the mortgage, then the list price should be:

$$list\ price = \frac{100{,}000}{.05} = 2{,}000{,}000$$

How does a real estate agent determine the Cap rate? They often factor in the state of the building and the risk involved in the area. Brand new buildings in affluent areas will drive a low Cap rate. Run down properties in the worst section of town will have a high Cap rate. That's how they're *supposed* to determine it, but in practice many Cap rates make no sense.

If you go into a conversation and ask, "What's the Cap rate?" you'll be immediately branded as a rookie. Anyone with experience won't ask this because she'll know that it's based upon the imagination of the agent. A more sensible question is "How many doors?" Note that this is the number of units and not the actual number of doors in the complex. Most neighborhoods have market "per-door" prices. Given a price and a number of doors, an investor will immediately have an idea whether it's a good buy.

Perhaps the only real use of a Cap rate is to estimate the profits when an inexperienced agent neglects to add the rents and expenses to the listing. In that case you can calculate

$$profit = list\,price \times Cap$$

In the example above, given a stated CAP of 7 percent and a list price of $2,000,000, we can calculate

$$profit = 2{,}000{,}000 \times .07 = 140{,}000$$

Now that you know the profit, you can estimate what the ROI might be. In this example the monthly payment for a $1,500,000 loan (75 percent of $2,000,000) with a 30-year term at 4.6 percent is $9,072. The yearly mortgage is therefore $108,864. Since the down payment is $500,000, we can calculate this ROI as

$$ROI = \frac{140{,}000 - 108{,}864}{500{,}000} = 6.2\%$$

Of course, since the agent didn't do the due diligence to include the information for you to calculate an actual ROI, you can't assume that she calculated the Cap rate correctly. Still, this provides a fair estimate that will allow you to decide whether to contact the agent for the true numbers. It also wouldn't be too far-fetched, given the listing will state the number of units and taxes are often in the listing or otherwise public, to estimate what the other expenses are and from that determine the current rents. Additional calculations can then reveal a guestimate of the pro forma ROI. Of course, it's usually easier to just call the agent.

Why Leverage Is Awesome

Before we move on to building ROI into our model, I need to diverge to discuss an important concept that the ROI formula makes very clear. It is always better to use leverage to purchase properties instead of paying cash. This is a controversial topic. I know many

Chapter 5

people, some of my clients among them, who refuse to take loans on properties. This is particularly common with buyers from other countries. Yes, I know I am one of them, but my husband knocked that out of me.

Let's say you have $500,000 to play with. We'll also say that the average per-door cost is $100,000 in your target area and that rents are $1,000 per month. Interest rates will be 4.5 percent for 30 years and the average total expenses are $400 per door per month for taxes, insurance, management, utilities, and so on. If you buy a five-unit complex (five units at $100,000 each is $500,000), how much will you make per year and what will your ROI be?

$$\text{net income} = (1000 - 400) \times 5 \times 12 = 36{,}000$$

Your profit will be $36,000 per year, and your ROI will be

$$\text{ROI} = \frac{36{,}000}{500{,}000} = 7.2\%$$

Now let's pretend you buy two buildings. You put 50 percent down ($250,000) on each building and so now you have ten units. The monthly mortgage at 4.6 percent will be $1,248 per month or $14,976 per year. Since you have two buildings, the total mortgage expense will be $29,952. Let's calculate your total income and ROI.

$$\text{net income} = (1000 - 400) \times 10 \times 12 - 29{,}952 = 42{,}048$$

$$\text{ROI} = \frac{42{,}048}{500{,}000} = 8.4\%$$

That's a bit better. You just "gave" yourself a $500 raise per month. Now what if you fully leverage and buy a total of twenty units? You'll put $500,000 down on a purchase price of $2,000,000. Your loan will be $1,500,000 and your monthly mortgage will be $7,689 or $92,268 per year. Let's see what happens to your total income and ROI.

$$\text{net income} = (1000 - 400) \times 20 \times 12 - 92{,}268 = 51{,}732$$

$$\text{ROI} = \frac{51{,}732}{500{,}000} = 10.3\%$$

Just by leveraging your money, you're making roughly $15,000 more per year. Some of you may not find that impressive, but let's see what happens if rents go up by $200.

First, let's see your total income with a single building:

$$\text{net income} = (1200 - 400) \times 5 \times 12 = 48{,}000$$

And now fully leveraged with twenty units:

$$\text{net income} = (1200 - 400) \times 20 \times 12 - 92{,}268 = 99{,}732$$

Just from using leverage, your income went from $48,000 to $99,732 and your ROI went from 9.6 percent to 19.9 percent. With leverage, you've created a virtual "fortress" against inflation! The longer you hold the buildings, the more likely the rents will increase. Your mortgage payments, however, will remain the same. In some of our own properties, rents have roughly doubled in three years since we've owned them. You can imagine how dramatic the difference is with leverage.

Banks like to loan you money. It's why they're there. Let them lend you money so you can enjoy more profits through leverage.

Calculating When to Sell

There's one more term I'd like to talk about before we finish this chapter. You won't find this in any other book because I made it up. I admit it's a bit of an advanced topic, but it's crucial to understanding when it might make sense to sell a property you own. I call it "Estimated Return on Investment" or eROI.

To calculate eROI, what you're going to do is the following:

1. Determine how much you would pull out if you sold your property today. This is calculated as

funds received = sales price − remaining principle − commissions − taxes

2. Calculate the net income per year you receive on your building *today*. This should be easy, since you know your loan payment and all expenses.
3. Take the number specifying how much money you would pull out from step one and find some example properties on the market you could purchase if you had that money. Calculate the resulting pro forma net income from that potential property. This is your eROI.
4. Divide the eROI from step three by the ROI from step two. This is your ratio of how much you can earn if you sell and put the funds toward a new property, compared to what you're earning today.

Let's say your property currently earns $50,000 per year. You bought it for $200,000 but it's now worth $400,000. You originally put down 25 percent or $50,000. Therefore, you have $250,000 in equity on the building ($200,000 in increased value plus your $50,000 down). If commissions and fees amount to 7 percent, then it will cost $35,000 to sell the building and you'll end up with $215,000.

You find a building that lists for $860,000, which you can buy with your $215,000 down, or 25 percent (how convenient!). If you calculate that this building will give you a net income of $100,000, then your ratio of eROI/ROI will be $100,000 divided by $50,000, or two.

What are you *really* calculating with these numbers? Imagine your money as workers. Each day you send out these workers to do their job, which is to earn you more money and hence hire more workers. They tend to get "bottled up" in buildings, though, so every now and then, you can sell that building and release them to bigger projects. What you're calculating here is how much more productive those workers will be if you do so.

My own logic for selling a building is complex, but I won't sell anything unless the ratio is at least two. However, I cannot emphasize enough that eROI *must* be calculated from *actual* buildings. You need to be absolutely confident that you'll earn more money from the transaction. Remember that if your building increased in value, so did many others. More than once, I've thought for sure I could gain by selling, only to find that prices had become so unreasonable in the area that I would gain little from the transaction.

For a real-world example, recall the single-family home I bought without my husband's knowledge that was earning $6,000 a year. We did a 1031 exchange (more on that in Chapter 16) into a thirty-unit building with a pro forma ROI of $120,000 per year. The current ROI was $6,000 a year and the eROI was $120,000 a year for a ratio of twenty. We would have had to have been braindead to not take that deal.

Return on investment is the magic number when it comes to evaluating properties. But what ROI should you seek? How does that *actually* factor into deciding whether to buy a building? For that, you'll need a model, which is the topic of our next chapter.

Chapter 6
Types of Investing

THIS IS THE second chapter among three that deal with the analytics of real estate. In the previous one you learned how to use math to evaluate one property against another. Our goal is to construct a model that will effectively determine which buildings you will buy. I'll discuss building that model in the next chapter, and in this one I'll discuss the different types of models.

When you boil things down, there are really two types of models. There are flips, where you buy a property, do some things to it or simply hold it for a short period, and then sell it for a profit. Then there are holds, where you buy a property, hold it for a while, and make money from the rents. Holds in turn can be divided into single family and multifamily, depending on how many families normally reside in the property. Single-family is then divided into houses and condos.

Investing in Flips

Let's discuss flips first. I know I've pretty much ignored them up to now. It's not that I don't find them lucrative. Indeed, they can be. The primary issue I have with flips is that they're not *always* lucrative. As the market changes, the viability of flips changes. Sometimes you can make a killing and sometimes you can lose your shirt. For those willing to get their hands dirty, they're certainly worth your attention.

There are entire books on flips, so I certainly don't recommend you go down that route with just this one. I'll provide a short summary of the important points in terms of evaluating them. In that respect, they're the same as multifamily. In each case, you're devising a model of what types of properties you want to buy. The only difference is what each model pertains to.

Before you even think of buying something to flip, you'll need to decide if you'll do the renovation work yourself, or if you want to hire someone. Your decision should depend solely on your capabilities and licenses, how much you want to make, and how much time you have. Doing the remodels yourself limits how many homes you can flip, but it also means lower labor costs.

Next, you need to decide what types of properties you want to flip. Some investors work in the luxury market. Others stick to condos and townhomes. Much of this will be restricted by your budget, but different types of homes require different skills. For example, you won't be working on a roof for a condo remodel. Likewise, that working-class home typically won't have architectural changes for a multi-nozzle walk-in shower system. If you're doing the work yourself, you likely have core experience in a specialty like plumbing, electrical, or structural engineering, and it may make sense to concentrate on properties where those skills give you an advantage over others without them. For example, other flippers may turn down that beautiful turn-of-the-century home with knob-and-tube wiring, but if you're an electrician or have the right people on your team, you may decide to tackle that challenge.

Calculating Profits for Flips

The next part of the model involves that math stuff again. To determine how much you can pay for a particular property, you'll need to estimate how much you'll make. There are two very different ways to go about this.

When I've flipped, I calculated as if I sold the property *today*. It's fairly easy to estimate what the property will sell for after the intended remodel simply by looking at comparative sales. The alternative is to calculate as if you sell the property *in the future*. That future is whenever you think the short hold or remodel will end.

The problem with calculating future value is that no one can accurately predict the future. What if you get the price wrong and bid too much? That can happen. I should also add that, if you're in a declining market, even a calculation based on today's value is risky. Personally, I would never flip in a declining market but I'm sure there are investors who have figured out how to make money there too.

To start, you're going to subtract the price you paid from the estimated property value when the remodel is complete. Next, you'll need to subtract other things, which we'll discuss below.

Most banks won't let you finance short-term projects like flips. That means you'll need a hard money loan. For what it's worth, not all hard money lenders have thugs on their payroll to break your legs when you don't pay. Most just repossess the property since that's more profitable given health insurance costs for thugs these days. Ideally, you should receive a recommendation and introduction from your agent.

In almost all cases, hard money loans require points up front and regular payments. A point is a single percentage of the loan amount, so if you borrow $100,000, then one point is $1,000. The loan may require payments of $1,000 or $2,000 every month. You'll need to estimate how many months the project will take, how long properties require to sell on the market, and how long they'll need to close.

If your hard money loan for $100,000 costs two points, plus one point each month, and you estimate the remodel will take three months, plus one month to sell and another month to close, then the loan will cost you a total of $7,000 ($2,000 in points plus $1,000 per month for five months). Hard money loan costs are a major expense in flips and therefore some flippers with deeper pockets choose to fund their own projects. Others decide to do the exact opposite and become hard money lenders for other flippers.

Next, you need to estimate the cost of the remodel. This is easily one of the most challenging aspects of flips, since an incorrect calculation could turn the profit margins red. Make sure to fix up a home only to the stage that it fits with the neighborhood. Going past the standards set by nearby properties will likely result in wasted funds. Also, a good rule of thumb is to add 10-20 percent over your project's expense estimate to the remodel costs.

You'll need to factor permitting fees into your expenses and the current inspection wait times into your timetable. Don't expect the city inspector to show up the day after you file for the permit because they're often booked weeks and occasionally months in advance. Do inquire about permitting fees ahead of time. Where we live, they're typically 10 percent of the cost of the work. That's never made sense to me since only marginally more work is required of the inspector, but that's how they're calculated.

You'll need to power and potentially heat or cool the property during the remodel. Therefore, make sure to factor in the utility bills. Taxes and insurance are other expenses often forgotten during estimates. Many insurance companies have packages for projects like flips. The taxes will usually be prorated for the time you have possession.

Finally, you should add real estate fees and staging costs. Don't look for a budget agent for flips. Remember that you have a lot of money on the line, and you need it handled by the best professional. Many consistent flippers become agents themselves to save on commissions. Just be careful about doing that. I've seen many cases where flippers went under due to real estate mistakes they made. A good agent should make the top priorities clear when undertaking a flip. Some will even give you a list of contractors who will do the work, if you don't have them. Perhaps the most important skill of the real estate agent, though, is predicting what the home will sell for once finished.

In terms of staging, would you ever have a party and serve the food the next day? Make the home look beautiful and market ready on day one. You'd think people would have the imagination to see how a space will work, but they don't. Prospective buyers need the staging to show them. Many homes are also cold and uninviting when empty. Adding a rug, minimal furniture and hanging pictures usually fixes that. There are professionals who specialize in staging and your agent should be able to recommend at least one.

Finally, you should have a professional photographer take pictures of the house. This is not an opportunity to show off your iPhone. There are specific ways a house should be displayed and a quality professional will handle this properly.

Calculating all of these costs is essential, along with predicting what the home will sell for. When you finally calculate what you should pay and place an offer or bid at auction, you'll compete with other buyers. Some may buy based on predicted future value, and if the property doesn't increase as much as intended, they'll lose money. While that sucks for them, you need to make sure to stick to *your* model, or you'll be the one stuck with a money-losing deal. Refer back to Chapter 1 for a cautionary tale. Many of the homes I foreclosed on were owned by investors who had too much at risk when the recession hit.

ROI for Flips

It's important to remember that ROI *does* apply to flips. All that money you expend in terms of a down payment on the hard money loan, the loan costs, remodel expenses, and other expenses detailed above, is held up for the duration of the flip. The main difference is that instead of calculating per year, you divide by the fraction of the year the money will be held up. So if a total of $400,000 was tied into a property that profited $50,000 over four months (one third of a year), then the ROI would be

$$\text{ROI} = \frac{50{,}000}{400{,}000} \times 3 = 37.5\%$$

This is all I'll say about flips in this book. I do feel they're a tool that all investors should know. Sometimes, holds turn into flips. We've done that ourselves with multifamily properties we initially intended to hold for a long period of time. While we were making great money on the rents, we couldn't overlook the fact that the properties had doubled or even quadrupled in value.

I should also note that it's possible to intentionally flip multifamily properties. In that case, you're renovating the complex and increasing the rents. Due to existing leases, most multifamily flips take at least a year. See Chapter 18 on value-add for more details on how to do this.

Investing in Holds

The other type of model, and the one I spend the most time on in this book because it works in both bear and bull markets, is the hold. In this case, you're trying to maximize the ROI of a property through rents.

I'll discuss this more in the next chapter, but you're going to construct a model of the ideal property you want to buy. This model will contain mathematical and physical constructs. The physical constructs are what your target property looks like.

The first decision you'll have to make is to choose between multifamily and single-family. Multifamily is our specialty, though we've bought single-family in the past. There's no right or wrong answer though, in my experience, multifamily typically generates more income. The economics were covered in the previous chapter when I discussed leverage. Simply put, the more units you can purchase with your money, the more you typically will make, and the better you'll be hedged against inflation.

Multifamily Buildings

Multifamily buildings are graded by letters – A, B, C, D, and F. The primary difference between this and grade school is that not everyone will want an A. These are brand-new shiny buildings where the furniture is so modern as to be completely useless and the tenants lift their chins extra high to avoid noticing the poor bastards groveling at their feet outside. These buildings are pretty, but they're also extremely expensive with sometimes negative ROIs (meaning you lose money every month).

Grade B is a fairly normal building where your average television character lives. Grade C is somewhat rough and is lower working class and public assistance tenants. Most people don't visit grade D buildings at night, and a tetanus shot is necessary after visiting grade F, assuming you survive. Most investors stick with B and C, but there's also "value add" to consider, which is a topic important enough to deserve its own chapter (Chapter 18).

Another major division within multifamily is residential versus commercial. Here, banks define a strict division. Residential is four units or less and commercial is five units or more. It matters most when you're applying for the loan. The loan for four units or fewer is similar to a single-family residential loan. The bank does factor

Chapter 6

in the rents, but whether you receive the loan, how much you must put down, and your interest rate will depend mostly on your own personal credit. In multifamily, the bank will treat the building as its own entity that must make money itself. Buying a multifamily building is closer to purchasing a business, which in truth is exactly what you're doing.

Which is better: commercial or residential? Here, it's really a numbers game. I can't answer this in a general sense because every property will be different. However, in my experience, commercial buildings tend to earn more due to economies of scale. Because you can manage large numbers of units together, the expenses tend to be lower per unit in a commercial property. To complicate matters, I've found that it's not strictly true that a larger building is more profitable than a smaller building.

Once a building reaches a certain size in units, significant changes are necessary in management. A forty-unit property usually doesn't need an on-site maintenance person. A one-hundred-unit property often does. That means you now have an additional salary on your books and therefore the hundred-unit property may be less profitable per unit than the forty-unit. Of course, as the units go up from one hundred, the numbers begin to look better until you need a second repairman, and then you'll need a permanent staffed office to collect rents, deal with tenant issues, and show vacant units.

The profitability of a multifamily building per unit looks more like a wave than an even incline. Profitability increases until you reach a certain level, after which there's a sharp decrease. It then increases steadily until another level, where there's another drop. If you do your numbers right, you'll ensure that each building makes sense. Never just assume that a larger building will earn more.

Although multifamily usually wins the profitability game, there are several reasons investors choose to invest in single-family instead. The primary contention is money. Multifamily buildings tend to cost more, and if you're limited in funds, single-family may be your only choice. This is especially true with condos, which I'll cover shortly.

In terms of commercial multifamily, which by definition is five or more units, experience can be a limitation. Banks *will not* lend money to you unless you have experience. That typically means you need to work your way up the chain by purchasing ever larger buildings, and successfully managing them. For that reason, you're not going to start out with a forty-unit apartment complex. Even if you can manage the down payment, as I write this book no bank that I know of will lend you the money.

Finally, there are personal inhibitions. It can be scary moving into multifamily as an investor. That's where the bigger investors and dragons live. For those used to the single-family market, there can be a great temptation to stay there. Personally, I find that foolish. Tenants in multifamily buildings share walls and roofs, reducing maintenance costs. The average maintenance cost on an equivalent number of single-family residences is therefore going to be higher. The economics almost always work in favor of multifamily.

Single-family Buildings

Now that I've sufficiently bashed single-family, let's talk about it. While I'm not in favor of investing in it long term, it's an excellent way for new investors to enter the field.

The absolutely most important thing, and I can't stress this enough when buying *any* property, but especially single-family residences, is to make sure you're cash positive. Calculate your ROI and make sure it's greater than zero. There are a lot of predatory agents and "experts" who sell you their classes and will tell you to buy on appreciation. Can you make money this way? Absolutely, many do. As long as the market keeps going up, you'll profit. But when it goes down, and it will, then it will destroy you. I've seen it. That's how I got my start in this business, by repossessing homes from investors who weren't cash positive and failed to read the market. Anyone who claims to read the market might as well sell you a bridge, too.

Keep in mind that this person who's trying to convince you to purchase a cash negative property is either making money from your purchase or is now primarily making money from training courses and not real estate. Don't fall for this. As long as your property remains cash flow positive, you can survive any downturn in the economy. If your building makes enough money, then you'll gather up a nest egg not only capable of weathering any storm, but also able to purchase others' properties, now on sale, whose owners failed to protect themselves.

So before you put that offer on a property for investment purposes, make sure you've calculated all your expenses and you're positive that you'll make at least *some* money every month.

Now let's discuss the absolute worst real estate investment—condos.

Investing in Condos

While condos are often the cheapest of properties to purchase, they tend to be horrible investments. They're really the worst of both worlds in that they house a single family and your investment prospects are dependent on the judgments of others.

When you own a condo, you're at the mercy of a homeowners' association (HOA). Do you like politics? An HOA puts all the drama of our national politics into a relatively small building. On occasion, it seems the smaller the building, the more everyone hates each other. HOAs can be extremely difficult to deal with and I wonder what percentage of condos are on the market simply because the owners can no longer deal with their HOA.

To start off, HOA bylaws can prevent you from renting out your unit. This is called a rental cap and each HOA works differently. A typical arrangement is that only a certain percentage of units can be rented at any one time. Each time a tenant leaves, you reenter the queue where you'll wait until you can rent out your unit again. You may be renting the condo without issues, only for a tenant to leave, when you'll learn that you cannot rent the unit anew because the cap has been reached. Your condo now stands vacant, though of course all mortgage payments, utility bills, and HOA fees remain due.

An HOA can also approve a special assessment for large improvements. Ironically, while many buyers and sellers hate special assessments, I like them. When done correctly (and that is a major assumption) large improvements can significantly raise the value of the building. If your unit is in a building with a special assessment, my recommendation is to wait for the work to be completed before selling. Right after a major upgrade, most condos see a corresponding increase in value greater than the special assessment. Also note that if you sell before the work is complete, most buyers will still expect the seller to pay off the assessment.

Nevertheless, you're at the mercy of the HOA for not only assessments, but also HOA fees. If your building has a pool and/or gym, these fees can be high. The HOA fees alone are the main reason I avoid condos as investments. You have to factor them into the ROI and, in most cases, they ruin it. Some buildings have fees much higher than the surrounding buildings, and purchasing a condo in such a building is a prime example of poor decision making. It's a simple fact that some associations are run better than others. When you buy a condo, you're betting that your HOA is smarter than others, but those dynamics constantly change with unit and HOA board turnover.

Conflicts between tenants can also be more extreme in condos, and there's usually nothing you can do about it. A friend once bought a condo and rented it out. The tenant had young children and the occupant in the unit below didn't like them stomping on the floor. My friend's tenant wasn't happy either, because the woman below smoked a lot, and the smoke rose through their vents.

What followed was an endless battle through the HOA and with lawyers. Several times my friend had to personally attend meetings held to resolve the issues, but there wasn't much she could do because she only owned that one unit in the building. Had she owned the building, she could have easily moved one tenant to another unit or, if the matter was serious enough, allowed one of the tenants to break their lease. I've done that many times to defuse situations.

Where Condos Make Sense

I think I've made my point that investing in condos sucks, but there are two situations where they still make some sense. The first I've already touched on: money. Condos tend to be the cheapest option for new investors, so this may be your only option. It's always better to invest than not invest if the numbers are positive. There's absolutely nothing wrong with buying a few condos to get your start in the industry, then move to houses or multifamily.

The other reason is less obvious. In my experience, during severe downturns in the economy, condos suffer the most. During recessions, condos can often be had for a steal. Although I'm not an economist, recessions tend to disproportionately affect the poorest people, and that means the condo market will be impacted more than single-family. Multifamily may also be affected, but usually class A and B are hit the worst because tenants move to more affordable options. When you get to class C, those are already the cheapest shelters possible. Rents may fall slightly, but everyone still needs a place to live.

Many of my clients have picked up units during downturns for as little as $30,000 and sold them for $150,000 or more when the economy improved a few years later. In the meantime, the numbers are well into the positive due to how little was spent on the purchase.

What's the moral of this story? I'll continue to harp on these two points throughout this book: Don't buy something that doesn't make financial sense and always make sure your ROI is positive. If you do that, you'll have capital available for when everything goes on sale.

I've now described the different types of investments available to you. In the previous chapter, you learned how to calculate ROI to evaluate one property against another. The next chapter will tie this all together to create a model you can utilize to make rapid decisions.

Chapter 7
Rapid Decisions

THE LAST TWO chapters have graduated you from newbie to real estate nerd. Now it's time to put together the math and facts into what I call a "model."

Imagine that you receive a phone call one day about an interesting property. The price is something you can barely afford. This may be the deal of a lifetime, or it could destroy you financially, you don't know which. Your agent has given you one hour to decide. There's no time to see it in person. From the information provided, which is a bunch of pictures, the rent roll, and the profit-loss statement - you need to make a call. So, what do you do?

Unless you've prepared for this moment you'll probably just cry a lot. Alternatively, you analyze/paralyze until either the time runs out or you decide you don't have enough data. Circumstances like these are why you build a model ahead of time. It states exactly what types of properties you're looking for. When a property comes your way, and the example above is very close to reality, you only need to determine whether it fits into your model.

Chapter 7

Preparing for Your Model

Making rapid decisions is a fact of life in real estate investments. There are a lot of people out there who want a good deal. The agent wants to sell the property, so she's not going to wait all day for your answer. In fact, there's a good chance she's not waiting already. Several other buyers are looking through the details at the same time. You'll need to quickly decide whether this property is something worth owning and, if it is, how much you are willing to pay. These calculations need to be solid because your agent is going to hold you to them. If you back out because you didn't properly run your numbers in the first place, there will be one dog in the yard who doesn't get any more bones.

Therefore, you're going to do all your homework ahead of time. Now some of you may still have PTSD from homework (I do), but this is the fun kind because instead of grades you get money, and you get more of it if you do your homework well. So what homework are you going to do?

You're going to visit possible areas where you might want to buy real estate. Talk with agents and *see* actual properties. While it's unlikely you'll see an apartment complex before you make an offer unless you live close to it, you will have a great idea of what properties look like in the area. Decide what kind of property you'd like to own, or more specifically, is there a type you *don't* want? Personally, I don't like cinder block. I've owned them before and made money but they're unsightly inside and out and therefore drive away good tenants, so they're not in my model. I'll discuss more about what to look for in an area and a building in the next chapter.

Physical Characteristics in Your Model

For question two of your homework, you'll decide what type of building you want. Are you looking for single-family or multifamily? How large of a building are you interested in? For multifamily, how many units does your ideal property have?

The answers will usually depend on your finances, and you'll often have a range. For example, lately I prefer buildings from twenty to seventy units. That doesn't mean I won't buy something out of that range, but that's where the gravy is for me.

How old of a building do you want? Some older buildings have additional plumbing and electrical concerns. Buildings built in certain years in the Pacific Northwest have siding issues. There's no right or wrong answer here, but you should have an idea of the age of a building you want to manage.

Similarly, you should target certain locations. Do you want to be in the best area of town or in the worst? Is there an up-and-coming neighborhood that you believe will transition? Usually, I have several locations in mind, along with places I know will be too expensive or too run-down. Again, there's no correct answer here. Everyone has their niche and you need to identify yours. What is your comfort zone?

Of course, the primary consideration is how much money you have to play with. Make sure to keep some aside for lender holdbacks, appraisals, and mortgage payments while you stabilize your new property. Talk with your lender to understand how much you'll need to put down, so you can then calculate how much building you can truly afford.

The Target ROI

After money, you'll need to devise a target ROI. That shouldn't be a random number from your head but should instead be based on the actual ROIs possible in the area. How much of a return do you expect from your investment? The target ROI is crucial because that allows you to remove your emotions from the decision.

I remember early in my career I noticed the cutest turn-of-the-century multifamily. It was adorable, with cute little windows, a hand-carved door, and regal decorative pillars. The property was in a historic district and was over a hundred years old. I just looked at the photo and fell in love. Joe ran the numbers and said he'd drive by it if I wanted, but there was no way by any stretch of the imagination he'd put an offer on it. The numbers made no sense.

The target ROI is there because you need to make money. That's why you're in this business. Numbers aren't cute. No one goes around saying, "Aw, isn't that the most adorable little nine! I just want to cuddle up and stare at it". Numbers are either greater, less than, or equal to other numbers. If the ROI of the property is more than your target ROI, then it's good. Otherwise, it's time to move on. There's nothing to see here.

Factors that Influence the Target ROI

What ROI should you target? That really depends on several factors.

> **Risk** – How much of a project do you want? Properties that bring higher ROIs are typically either projects, in rougher areas, or both. I'll discuss this further in Chapter 18 but, especially if you're new to investing, you may want something that's just turnkey.
>
> **Area** – Certain geographies are just more expensive than others. Even within a single metro area, ROIs vary widely. In general, the better the neighborhood the lower the ROI, because the areas already generate a lot of investment due to being a better known "brand". Personally, I stick mostly to working-class neighborhoods. These lack the more extreme problems of rough neighborhoods but provide a much better ROI than wealthier areas.
>
> This can be counterintuitive to many new buyers because in single-family properties, the trend for price increases favors those nicer

neighborhoods. When things are good, prices tend to increase the most in wealthier areas, even by percentage. Rents, however, tend to stay behind and usually the rent for your average two-bedroom unit in the nicest neighborhood won't be that much more than the corresponding rent in a working-class neighborhood.

For example, in the area where I live, a nice 2 bed unit in a great town at the time I'm writing this will rent for roughly $2,800 per month as compared to $1,800 per month in the working-class towns a half hour south. A duplex will sell for $1,500,000 in the first neighborhood as compared to $600,000 in the second. You don't need to be a genius in math to tell which one has the better ROI.

Partners – I'll discuss partners more in Chapter 12, but I seek a higher ROI when I know I'll have to involve someone else. Why? Because I'm a chicken. I don't want to have to explain to an investor why the property isn't making money for the first year. I also don't want to explain the tough choices necessary to turn a "value add" building around, which often means replacing every tenant and taking a loss for a few months. A higher ROI will reduce the odds that I have to have those uncomfortable discussions. For buildings I own completely, I'll accept a lower ROI because I'll have full control over my actions.

Market – As areas become more popular, real estate rises in price. Rents will usually increase too, but not as dramatically. I've seen this happen in many neighborhoods. Prices are very reasonable until the city lands on a few short lists in "best places to invest" publications, and suddenly there's a rush. Per-door asking prices will increase until Wall Street and the syndicates take notice, and then they'll skyrocket.

Potential Competitors Who Will Outbid You

I'll go into more depth in Chapter 12, but be aware that syndicates and financial institutions use far different models from those I've outlined here; theirs are typically more dependent on property values increasing than on the ROI from rents alone. They're therefore more immune to higher prices that may result in losses, or at least the institutions who manage them are, since the investors will take the brunt if things go south.

This last remark about syndicates raises a crucial point. The reason you have a model is to identify properties you would like in your portfolio. Your model is like a bouncer at a bar who determines if you're cool enough to get in. *Trust your model.* That's why you took so many pains to put it together. When you're in a hot area, you *will* be outbid by syndicates and other individuals with different financial goals. A syndicate is a voracious monster that eats real estate. Its managing partners primarily make money when they acquire and finance an asset. Because of this, they're far more willing to pay amounts that make no sense from an ROI viewpoint. They have far different financial motivations, and are likely to outbid you.

In addition to syndicates, some markets are popular with foreign investors who just want to park their money. Funds left in their home country might be subject to seizure by the government, so they need to get them out. They don't care as much about ROI through rents. They instead concentrate primarily on the ease of future liquidation. For that reason, they tend to focus on the best neighborhoods with the best schools, because these properties should always be in high demand. If you try to compete with these investors, you will lose, and that's fine. Just lick your wounds and move on.

An Example Model

Here's a model that we've used: *Our ideal property should be between four and twelve units in either southern King County or northern Pierce*

County of Washington State. It should not be cinder block and should be built later than 1980. The neighborhood must have a below average incidence of crime unless it's close to downtown Tacoma, because we believe that area's transitioning upwards. Our target ROI is 20 percent and our minimum ROI is 18 percent.

Those of you thinking that I just gave a hot tip should understand that I long ago moved on from this model. The areas near downtown Tacoma have since transitioned – as I predicted - and an ROI approaching 18 percent is practically impossible now. Our models have changed over time, as will yours.

Your model is your protection. It will save you from all the unsavory characters who are just trying to take advantage of you and your money. Now that I've explained the use and importance of the model, it's time to detail how to use it.

Using Your Model to Evaluate a Property

Let's imagine that your agent has sent you an OM or Offering Memorandum. This is an advertisement, so treat it as such and just pick out the numbers and pictures. The memorandum will also contain a blurb about the area, comparable sales that justify the price, and comparable buildings that validate the pro forma rent. If you've done your homework, you can ignore all these things. You should already know these details. I must point out that I cannot recall the last time the pro forma rents in a memorandum were correct.

The very first thing I run are the numbers. That's because the ROI is my most neutral gatekeeper, and if the numbers don't make sense, then it's a no-go. Where do you find the numbers for the ROI?

The document you seek is called a T-12, often included in the Offering Memorandum or else requestable from the seller. This isn't a Terminator model; it's a spreadsheet containing the income and expenses for the most recent year. In Chapter 5, I outlined which fields should concern you most. Keep in mind that it's rare you can accept the figures in a T-12 at face value. Everyone runs their numbers differently, and you should keep an eye out for the following:

Beware of loss to lease. This is just a tricky way of saying the rents aren't what they say they are. You must deduct the loss to lease from the rents to know what they're actually receiving. We covered loss to lease in Chapter 5.

Some utilities aren't paid every month. That's where a T-12 is useful as compared to a report covering only the last three months. Over a twelve-month span you can more accurately calculate what the utility costs are per year.

Ignore the management costs if you intend to replace the management with your own, which I recommend. Of course, when the property manager is showing you the building during walk-through or inspection, don't tell her that.

You should have already decided how you want to handle maintenance costs as detailed in Chapter 5. The challenge here is that they vary widely from month to month and even year to year. A roof replacement, for example, can greatly skew the costs for a year.

Another document you'll receive is the rent roll. I generally only glance through it. The T-12 should list the average rent per unit type, which is really what you want to know. The rent roll also provides a total count of vacant units, how often tenants pay late, how many tenants have pets, and makes clear any special situations. Often, you'll find one or more tenants with rents significantly lower than others. You should ask the seller through your agent the reason for these. Valid cases are lowered rents because the tenant performs on-site maintenance, cleanup, and property showings. Sometimes the seller just feels sorry for or favors specific tenants. Beware of those tenants, because they're more likely to react badly to new management and you'll probably have to replace them.

Another thing to check on the rent roll is the leases. It's important to know how many are month-to-month. For those who have leases, when do they end? Note that it's a good practice to state in the contract that the buyer must approve all new leases and extensions. Too often, sellers or their property managers will sign a two-year lease for a ridiculously low rent a week or two before the sale closes. Some can be challenged in court, but that in itself is a hassle.

As mentioned in Chapter 5, in a pinch you can estimate the ROI from the CAP rate. You should *never* rely on this alone for an offer, but if all you have is an online listing, it should be enough to justify contacting the agent for the T-12 and rent roll.

Finalizing the Decision

Once the property has gone through the "ROI gate" it's time to evaluate the other aspects. I'll detail most of these in the next chapter, but here I'll stress that you're going to check the property against the standard you've devised in the model. Ultimately, if the numbers make sense you're going to ask yourself, "Is this the type of building I want to own?"

If your answer is yes, then buy it immediately. Seriously, don't wait around on it. There are a lot of other investors out there. If you know you want the property, then do not pass Go. Do not stop for Starbucks. Go straight to your agent (but call her. She won't like it if you stand outside her house) and tell her to write an offer. Tell her for how much and verify her thoughts on whether that will be enough. Too many times I've seen clients dink around on a property, only to lose it because someone else made a move faster.

That's why you have a model. You built it yourself. You trust the model. Your model is awesome. It's the secret weapon in your laptop that enables you to move at lightning speed like Alexander the Great across Persia. It's what enables you to be fast, decisive, and serious.

Competing with Others

Let's assume that you're on the phone with your agent now. You've told her you want the property. You expect to hear that the seller loves your offer. This is just such a perfect match and you'll be so happy together! Only that's not the response. "They have other offers," she'll say. Everything comes crashing down. That euphoric life of sipping margaritas at the beach while your bank account bulges is gone. You're not even at the altar yet and already your building is cheating on you. How could this happen? What do you do now?

Your model should be tugging at your shoulder. That good old dependable model knows what to do. Remember when you decided on a target ROI? Well, you should also have a minimum ROI. Below that value the deal doesn't make sense. Now you're going to fiddle with the sales price until you're right *at* your minimum ROI. That's the maximum you should pay.

Now is the time for a serious talk with your agent. Let her know what your maximum is, then ask what she thinks will get the property. Sometimes it's not only about the money. In the commercial world especially, the strength of the buyer matters. Ultimately what the seller wants most is for the building to sell. A higher offer won't matter if the buyer has a history of backing out of deals. Remember all those times I told you to be a good dog? This is where you earn the bone.

Other times, the contract terms could be the differentiator. The seller may be interested in a quick closing. Perhaps the seller wants the buyer to assume a loan to avoid a prepayment penalty. In some small properties where the owners have grown attached to the tenants, they may want some assurances the tenants will be cared for. You need your agent to ask what the seller wants.

If it's money, though, then don't be cheap by trying to hold to a lowball offer. If the numbers still make sense, put your best foot forward. That's easily the best way to tell the seller how much you want the property. These days, sob stories about how you've always wanted a sixteen-unit apartment complex and need room to expand from your current eight-unit just aren't going to work.

Of course, sometimes another party's bid comes in higher. This is where you need to stick to your guns. Don't let it get emotional. It's perfectly fine to lose a property. Remember that your goal is to make money. As I've already mentioned, not every investor shares your goal. Not everyone can accurately price a property and not everyone goes strictly by ROI. Your agent may push you to raise your offer, but as long as you're being realistic about the market, you should wait.

Adjusting Your Model

If you happen to notice a pattern where you're either constantly outbid or nothing pencils out to your ROI target, then you have a problem. It's very likely your model is no longer realistic. Your target ROI should be possible to achieve and must be based on actual buildings. These can't be buildings that sold a year ago when the market was completely different. Your numbers need to be achievable.

Should you then offer more on that property? No. Your model is at fault, not the property. Go back and examine recently sold listings and others on the market now. If your ROI is only slightly off, then you may just need to wait. However, if nothing is tracking anywhere near your target, then you need to reevaluate things again.

When reevaluating, you need to understand something that no real estate agent wants you to know: You don't *have* to buy something just to buy something. At times the market takes turns that don't make sense. Purchasing a property just to get something in your portfolio can be very dangerous.

If your model was constructed with prudence and care, then the fact that everything's priced out of your model may tell you it's not time to buy. It may also be telling you that it's time to try something new.

We witnessed this ourselves in the Seattle market. At the time, we owned roughly twenty units and wanted to expand, but the area had become hot and even the working-class neighborhoods didn't pencil out. Prices just kept going higher and higher without the corresponding jumps in rents (which were increasing, but not by as much). Instead of purchasing multifamily, we switched to a few single-family homes in an area that I felt was very underpriced.

I was correct, as they roughly doubled in price over the next year, and by that time I'd identified another state with numbers that easily exceeded my target ROI. By that time, I had a decent amount of cash to play with and was more than ready to perform.

Now you have your model and you're ready to start searching. Let's get out in the field and discuss what makes a good building.

Chapter 8

Identifying Properties

IT'S TIME TO look past the numbers. What makes a good investment building? To start, remember the old saying: location, location, location. There's a reason it's repeated three times. No other aspect is going to affect your bottom line more. The trick, of course, is finding a good location.

The Neighborhood

The best areas for investment aren't often where you'd expect. As previously mentioned, the most affluent parts of town are usually the worst for ROI. They *can* be great places for speculation, since when the market is good, growth there tends to be the best, but when the market turns, you could be in real trouble.

On the opposite side of the spectrum, you need to be wary of the worst neighborhoods. Sure, bad neighborhoods can be good investments given the right conditions—more about that soon—but you need to be careful because many of them don't get better. For example, the city near where my husband grew up was depressed and a poor investment when he was a child. Now, many years later, it's roughly the same.

Not long ago, I was foolish enough to put an offer on a building in a city we hadn't visited. Sure, we had discussions about the area with our agent and understood it to be up-and-coming. I put in an offer and flew out for the inspection. While the building itself was as advertised and the pro forma numbers I calculated seemed doable, I was disturbed by a drive through the neighborhood. Every other house was either vacant or burned to the ground. People weren't walking on the street.

Maybe that area was in line for a turnaround, but I didn't see it. For some distance around, things were depressing. When I video called a friend who was more street-smart than I am, he told me to immediately get the f* out of there.

When I showed my videos of the neighborhood to Joe, he was concerned that, even if the area turned around, there was too much vacant land and project homes in the area. In other words, these abandoned homes and burned-out properties would be replaced with buildings that would *compete* with ours. A little competition is normally a good thing, but not when there's so much real estate available.

We backed out of the deal and I'm still puzzled why I didn't follow my own advice and investigate the neighborhood first. Due to the stunning ROI, though, and the city's proximity to my other investments, I thought it should work. I was wrong.

Evaluating Jobs and Housing Availability

The key with "challenged" neighborhoods is that there needs to be some hope. Are more jobs moving to the area? What is the likelihood that your tenants will get those jobs?

In another situation, which I brought up earlier, I learned that Toyota was building a massive factory in a new town. That meant a lot of jobs. There were other projects in the works, too. Two government agencies were building headquarters in the same city. Other car manufacturers had announced projects and the city and state were making a huge investment in a new industrial area. The properties at hand were in challenged neighborhoods but I knew there were a lot of new jobs on the way.

Another important step when investigating new areas is to research availability. Look online for how many people are looking for places, and then check how many listings there are. Look at how many views the listings have. Even more important, go to that neighborhood, stop for a bite to eat at a restaurant or café, and ask your waiter how easy it is to find rentals and what kinds of jobs are coming to town. Repeat that for lunch and dinner. Let them talk and you'll have all the information you need.

Take the neighborhood targeted by Toyota as an example. I knew jobs were coming. Was there enough housing to accommodate them? Some quick research and discussions with locals indicated the answer was an emphatic *No*. Sure, there were several housing developments going up, but most people moving into the area for manufacturing jobs wouldn't be able afford them.

When I learned of the sharp increase in jobs combined with the limited housing, I knew it was a good buy. I wasn't the first to realize that. Multifamily prices had already increased sharply and the per-door prices had roughly doubled in the last two years. However, simple ROI calculations showed there was still a lot more room both for property prices and rents to rise. Pro forma ROIs were calculating at 30 to 40 percent.

If you see these numbers, you should move, and move fast. My calculations and estimates proved correct. Rents in the area have almost doubled and per-door prices are roughly triple what we paid for our first buildings. The area is now consistently ranked among the best in America for real estate investment and for quality of life, but ironically the ROIs have plummeted and I recently decided to hold back on new acquisitions there. It's still a great place to own, but with the higher purchasing prices, the majority of sales now go to Wall Street firms and syndicates.

What the Numbers Won't Tell You

Sometimes, a good neighborhood isn't as obvious as you'd think. For example, I was offered a building in a small town about forty-five minutes from Seattle. When I researched jobs, the results were dicey. The town had a few employers, but they were in manufacturing and in risky areas. With technology moving the way it was, they could become obsolete at any time. Most of my potential tenants worked in those factories.

On the housing side, things looked better because available housing was scarce. I spoke to several locals (bartenders, waiter's etc., see the pattern?) and the housing problem they described was severe. That piqued my interest.

The building was in a bad section of town. However, a stop at the police department revealed that the property under consideration was the cause of the crime. Pretty much every drug dealer in town lived there. It was a small town. Everyone knew the building one way or another.

When I thought about it, I realized the local jobs didn't matter as much. The town was still within striking distance of Seattle which had tons of jobs and no affordable housing. *If you buy it, they will come.*

So we bought it. The sheriff removed a few drug-dealing tenants shortly before we took possession, and I turned it around. I'll detail more about this in Chapter 18 about value-add, but I was absolutely correct about the jobs. Once the building was fixed up, I was able to rent the units to tenants who worked in Seattle.

Besides asking about jobs and housing, it's worth some time to investigate online. BestPlaces.net offers interesting statistics about each city in the U.S. and provides a way to compare them. While most of these numbers come from old data, they do paint a general picture. Note that most published data is old. In fact, I often have a laugh at our local newspaper, since whenever they post an article about the market, their statements *were* true a month or two ago but are no longer so.

Calculating Rents

Once you have a location and an agent, you'll start receiving notices of properties for sale. Besides checking their ROIs, how can you evaluate them? How can you be sure you've calculated the right pro forma ROI?

In terms of calculating pro forma rents, it's a good idea to consult several sources and combine them. Your property manager will be the primary source, but unless you have a strong relationship with that manager already, his numbers may not be correct. Keep in mind that some property managers price units below market value. They're typically paid for each tenant placed in addition to the standard rates, so they have financial incentives to fill units quickly, and even to cycle tenants. Of course, once you have a manager you fully trust, this will be your primary source.

Websites like HotPads.com can serve as additional sources. You need to find a site that includes actual listings. Don't pay attention to aggregators like Rentometer; They're more often incorrect and their numbers are based on old data. Make sure the buildings and units are similar to yours and beware that expanding your search radius by even a mile or two can bring up vastly different neighborhoods.

Once you have a target rent in mind, play devil's advocate and consider how practical it will be to increase the rents to that target. This is when you need to double check the leases. If a tenant just signed a two-year lease, you'll have to wait two years before you can raise their rent. Month-to-month tenants, on the other hand, can be raised right away. I'll cover how to raise rents in Chapter 13.

Now is also a good time to double-check local regulations. I hope you checked them already when investigating locales, but you need to understand your restrictions when deciding how easy it is to raise rents. For example, in the city of Seattle, property owners are currently required to give tenants a 180-day notice of a rent increase. In certain circumstances, the landlord must pay moving expenses for tenants. The reasons for evictions are highly restricted and no evictions, under any circumstances, may take place between November and March. How do we deal with it? We don't. Joe and I sold all our properties there long ago, and if you do invest in such an area, I recommend getting to know an attorney who specializes in landlord-tenant laws.

Tenant Amenities

Besides laws, you should check tenant amenities. While some complexes have clubhouses, gyms, and swimming pools, all of which I prefer to call liabilities, all properties will have some form of parking associated with the property, even if that's just streetside parking and there's no actual parking spots on the property itself. In a downtown environment, you may be able to get away with not having a parking story, but in most locales that will seriously reduce your clientele. Parking can be a huge issue for tenants and the lack of it is a major turnoff. Make sure you have ample spots for all your tenants and keep in mind that the occupants of many two-bedroom units will have two cars.

Washers and dryers are another tenant amenity. Does each unit have one or are they in a common area? People tend to have clothes and prefer to wash them. Make sure you have a solution available. If your intention is to provide washers and dryers in each unit, be sure to walk through the floor plan with a contractor to verify that's possible. Your contractor will need to check for adequate plumbing and electrical outlets, while also heeding local codes and common sense. I once passed on a building when confronted with the fact that I couldn't add washers and dryers. The property was in a nice area, but to justify the higher rents I needed, tenants would expect in-unit hookups.

Does the property have free internet or cable for tenants? Well, that sucks for you. It's rare to obtain a corresponding increase in rent, so those are mostly income eaters.

Besides adding laundry capabilities, what other improvements will you have to make? Does the building require a paint job on the interior or exterior? What's the status of the roof? Do you need new floors and windows? How much will all these repairs cost?

Estimating Repairs

There are two basic types of repairs to a property: those you do right after taking possession and those you do afterwards. At purchase time, you're most concerned with those you'll need to do immediately. Basic unit remodels can usually be done afterwards and, if you plan things well, can be paid for by rental income. However, if there's a tree parked in the center of your building after a storm and a quarter of the units are no longer habitable, then you'll need to handle that sooner. By the way, don't laugh at the tree remark. That actually happened to me.

If you can, bring a contractor out to the property. Walk through it together to look for high-level problems and estimate how much they're going to cost. Note that many times this will only be possible after placing the offer as sellers aren't keen to have random buyers walking around. For residential duplexes and fourplexes, though, this sometimes is allowed.

Whatever you do, please don't add up every light switch and doorknob. These are trivial expenses and not worth your worries. You're after the big things, perhaps $1,000 and up. Keep in mind that at this stage you don't need an accurate estimate, you just need a ballpark figure to determine whether the numbers still work.

Perhaps even more important than the repair cost estimate is the knowledge of what you're getting into. Is this a big project? Are many of the units stripped down to the studs and will require major work and permitting? Perhaps you're up to such a challenge, and perhaps you're not. There's nothing wrong with rejecting a building because you know the amount of work will stress you out too much. I've drawn my line plenty of times.

Estimating Maintenance

Besides the obvious things you may need to repair, such as the roof and windows, there are also maintenance hassles. In the South, you'll need to pressure wash any building with siding regularly, at least every other year. The following are other items that may matter, though this is far from an exhaustive list.

Chimneys and fireplaces can incur major expenses. Birds may nest in chimneys. If the fireplaces are still active, they and the chimneys will need to be regularly inspected for fire dangers.

The exterior of the building matters. In the Pacific Northwest, LP siding can be a major issue. Cinder block can cause moisture issues and putting siding over it may be expensive and require a permit.

What about the foundation? Post-and-pier can suffer from ventilation and moisture problems. A crawl space may become the hottest rat joint in town. Concrete foundations have fewer of these problems but can easily quadruple the cost of any repair work.

In multi-story buildings, pay attention to the outside entries. Are the stairwells in the interior or exterior? You will be responsible for maintaining stairwells. You'll need to regularly paint, light, and floor those spaces. Exterior entries offer different concerns because they're subject to weather. Wooden platforms will suffer rotten boards and will have to be replaced at some point. Metal platforms last longer but need to be painted to avoid rust.

None of these features should prevent you from purchasing a building, but they need to factor into your maintenance expenses. If you see high repair expenses in the property financials and there are a number of warning signs on the exterior, then you'll need to consider whether the higher maintenance costs will prevent you from achieving your target ROI.

At some point, with some building, you're going to run the numbers and find them within your target ROI. The building parameters will match those in your model. The location will be awesome, with plenty of future jobs and not so much housing. You'll look at the property, and things will seem pretty good.

"I can do this," you'll say to yourself, and you'll be right. You'll be able to handle this property because you've done your homework. You've known all along what you were looking for, and this is it.

You're calling your agent now to write it up. Welcome to the rat race. Let's get started with that offer.

Chapter 9
The Contract

Great! You've found the real estate investment of your dreams, or at least one that will make you money, and are anxious to make an offer. Here's the first question: Who's going to write it?

Deciding Who Will Write the Offer

Your choices will vary greatly, depending on whether the property is residential or commercial. Recall that residential is one to four units, and commercial is anything larger than that. They are complete opposites in terms of who should write it.

For residential, you should ideally have your own agent representing your interests. There are agents who "double dip," meaning they frequently represent both the seller and the buyer when drawing up the contract, and you should run away from them. Why? Because they're getting paid twice without truly representing one party's interests. In most cases, if you're looking at a residential investment your choice will be easy: use the same agent who's been guiding you through the process and helping you find something to write the contract. If you use a residential agent for finding commercial properties, she will expect to write them, and if a residential agent has the listing, the process is no different for buying a commercial property

In the commercial world, it's the exact opposite. Yes, you typically will have an agent you work most closely with, and at times she will write an offer for a property she didn't list, but most of the time she'll be writing up an offer on one of her own listings.

Say, what? This is where the dragons are. It's the way the game is played. Many if not all commercial agents will only send you their own listings. Occasionally they'll send you something from a seller who hasn't signed a listing agreement with them yet, and that's because they're trying to tease an offer from you to justify the listing.

If you remember what we learned in Chapter 3, you'll recall that I advised you to research who lists the interesting buildings. This is why. You want to remove every obstacle to getting those properties, and never even seeing the listing is a very big obstacle.

Your Mindset for the Offer

Secondly, before you contact your agent to put in that offer, make sure you really want it. Yes, things come up. You may not have realized that 80 percent of the units are meth labs. You may not have known that no floors exist on the interior and the property is uninhabitable except by an advanced species of cockroach. However, if the inspection confirms that the property is roughly what was advertised, you need to follow through and buy it. Don't be wishy-washy. Those dogs don't get the bones and you'll be quickly sleeping out in the rain.

Think about it from the seller's viewpoint. They just want top dollar for their property, and they want it to close. They've hired your agent to do that. Your agent, in turn, knows you. She's looked at your finances, your experience, and has a pretty good idea how serious you are. That agent is going to select the best offer in both price and likelihood to close among those competing. Numerous times, I've won a property without being the strongest offer. They looked instead at my other qualities. I'd demonstrated previously that I would close. I knew the area and had other properties nearby. I'd completed similar projects.

Now here's the kicker. Your commercial agent isn't going to represent your interests. I bet you're not feeling well right now. Of course, your agent is double dipping, but she's not going to bargain down the seller after inspection. Oh, you're upset? That's why you're reading this book. *You* are the only person you can trust to act in your interests, and I wrote this book to explain how to do that.

If you feel after inspection that something previously unknown will cost a significant amount to remedy, it will be up to you to negotiate with the seller through your agent for that amount. No one else will do it.

Determining the Purchasing Entity

Once you've decided who will write the offer, you need to figure out who will buy it. That may seem obvious but thinking it through carefully can save you thousands or even millions later on.

While everyone's situation is different and you'll need a CPA who specializes in real estate to discover what's best for you, in most cases the right answer is an LLC. An LLC, or Limited Liability Corporation, is a small corporation, often composed of just yourself, without most of the reporting and paperwork of what you may typically think of as a corporation. There are entire books written about them. At the time I'm writing this, an LLC has the best tax advantages, and in some cases helps to protect your personal assets. The real question is how to purchase a property under one.

For commercial buildings over four units, you can simply purchase the property under the LLC. You're essentially buying a business with a business, and that's fairly straightforward. Sometimes, though, you may not know which entity you'll place it under when you write the offer. Since it takes a bit of time to incorporate, you probably won't want to wait for that process to be finished before writing your offer. Luckily, you don't have to.

The following are the procedures for buying a property when the purchasing entity isn't known in advance.

- In the offer, put something similar to this as the buyer: "(your name) John Doe and or assign." Essentially, you're saying that you are buying it and will assign it to some other entity that you'll create for this building once you're under contract. In a commercial world, it's a common practice and most sellers won't care.
- Have your attorney write up the articles of incorporation for your LLC or business entity.
- File your paperwork in the appropriate state. Again, a CPA or attorney who specializes in real estate can provide the best advice here. Many investors incorporate in states such as Nevada or Delaware instead of their home state.
- Once you've incorporated, have your agent fill out an addendum to the purchase and sale agreement of the property stating, "Buyer's name shall be as follows (your new entity name)."
- Have all parties sign off on it, and send copies to escrow, the closing attorney, title, and your lender.

Note that while a good agent will help you get this done, the job belongs to you. Make sure all parties are aware of the correct name.

Residential Contracts

Residential and commercial real estate contracts differ significantly. Complicating matters is that either contract may be followed if both parties agree.

Residential contracts are typically used for up to four units, but on occasion may also apply for slightly larger buildings if both agents have residential backgrounds. The contract format for a residential purchase is well-defined, and most agents use templates and fill in the blanks. The contract spells out things such as inspection and financing periods, the procedure to follow for remedies after inspection, and various clauses that are detailed ad nauseum online. In short, if you've ever purchased a home before, you'll find the experience familiar.

The following are some good guidelines to follow when submitting a residential offer. Note that every sale is different and practices vary by area.

Inspection – You should typically have five to ten days to schedule and complete your inspection. Any more and the seller will believe you're wishy-washy. In very hot markets, the seller may provide a pre-inspection report. They will expect you to waive your inspection contingency if you're satisfied after reading it.

Financing contingency – This is twenty days in a normal market. In a hot market, you might waive this if you're fully approved and underwritten.

Title contingency – This should be three to five days, though in a hot market this will likely be reviewed prior to the offer and waived. You may be alarmed at waiving so many things, but when there are a lot of other offers, you need ways to make yours stand out and present yours as serious. Waiving contingencies are only necessary when there's a lot of competition in the market.

Earnest money – 1 to 5 percent of the purchase price is normal. Higher amounts can occur, though they're often accompanied by contract language that limits what the seller can keep in the case of default.

Closing date – Your agent should call the listing agent and ask what the seller wants. Thirty days is typical for residential sales. Sometimes the seller will ask to rent back for a period, though this is much less common in residential investments than in single-family homes. In those cases, thirty to sixty days of rent back is not unheard of. Just be aware that the sellers will become your tenants and will be subject to all landlord-tenant laws.

Again, your agent should guide you through the terms necessary to win the property, but the above should give you an idea of the possibilities.

Commercial Letters of Intent

Commercial contracts are a different beast. First, they start with a letter of intent (LOI). This is a relatively informal document that states the purchase price offered, the due diligence period, and how long it should take to close. Often, it's only one page, and it's not a legally binding contract. If we can compare purchasing a commercial property to dating, this step is kind of like a little note expressing interest and asking if they like you too.

How the sellers and their agent respond to the LOI will vary. In the residential world, there are strict laws that stipulate all offers must be shown to the seller and possibly restrict what information they may be shown. For example, some states and cities outlaw buyer "love letters" that detail who the buyers are and why they want the property so badly. In the commercial world, these love letters are typically ignored.

At times, the seller may ask you to walk the property. Since it's typical for an LOI to be written with the property sight unseen, they'll want to make sure you're truly interested. Sellers may also request a phone call with prospective buyers. During such calls, the buyers are expected to explain their interest in the area and the subject property and, just as important, their current holdings and experience in the area and in similar buildings.

Sometimes there is no time limit for responding to an LOI. Commercial real estate is more of a Wild West, so it takes as long as it takes. Both parties are aware that the other may back out if something more interesting appears. A good agent should keep pressure on the seller to respond, and if the commercial agent represents both sides, she'll be very motivated to encourage the seller to do so. However, you'll need to be patient.

Reasons for the seller delaying their response could be the time needed to get all parties to agree in the case of an estate, debate within a syndicate or with silent partners, or the sale might simply not be a high priority for this seller. Keep in mind that if you're buying in a different state, customs may vary from what you're used to. For example, I've found that in the deep South sometimes there's no real hurry in such matters.

Reasons You May Lose

Eventually, the sellers will decide whose offer to take. While you hope it's yours, the following are reasons yours may not be chosen.

- Money is the most common reason. Someone gave a much sweeter offer. If you could have offered more while staying within your target ROI, well… don't do it again!
- Someone else offered better terms. Sellers like cash. If you're financing and someone else is paying cash, and the amounts are similar, then you're going to lose. You can eliminate this flaw while still financing by using hard money. It's a risky choice since you'll have holding costs (see below) and refinancing could take longer than you think.
- Another party is more qualified than you are. In this case you simply lost out to a bigger dog.

- The agent sold the property to one of her own buyers. In commercial, you should have had the listing agent write it up.
- The listing agent was more familiar with another buyer. This happened to us on our first out-of-state property. We had the highest offer, but we were unknown to both parties. Remember that the agent and seller both want the property to close, and without a track record, they have no idea if you'll do so. We lost that first property, but a few weeks later we offered on another and got it.

Hard Money Loans

I feel it's necessary at this point to discuss hard money loans for purchasing properties. Similar to hard money loans for financing flips (see Chapter 6), some person or company lends you the money instead of a bank, usually for a much higher interest rate and for a short period of time. The primary difference between hard money loans here and those for flips is the duration. This is often brought up, especially in the commercial world, when a building either has high vacancies or is in bad shape. The problem buyers run into with such properties is many traditional banks won't have an appetite for them. While there are rehab loans, they can be tricky to obtain and closing may take eons, since the bank will want to know exactly what is necessary to stabilize the property.

Some agents will strongly recommend approaching a hard money lender. The advantages to the agent and seller should be obvious: the building will close quickly. As a buyer, you should be very, very cautious.

The first consideration is simply money. You'll pay one or two points (each point is 1 percent of the loan amount) up front, and typically one point each month thereafter. You'll have to factor this into your price.

More serious is that this allows you to purchase a building that may never be habitable. Banks will require appraisals, surveys, sometimes environmental and seismic reports, and may send someone to inspect major work. A bank won't finance a building that has some irredeemable quality, but hard money lenders take far fewer precautions.

Your target building may be ready to fall into the ocean. The seller secretly knows that and wants you to take a hard money loan so it will become your problem. No bank will ever finance that property because their appraiser and inspectors will tell them the building is about to fall into the ocean. Now you're stuck with a property that will eventually be inhabited by fish and crabs, none of whom will pay rent.

We once had a building on contract that had taken major damage during a windstorm. We stipulated that the sellers had to complete the repairs (their insurance had already given them the money to do so), but they were lagging behind schedule. When we showed up on site to inspect the current state of the property ourselves, we became suspicious of the work. Finally, with the job moving at molasses speed, the seller asked us to just get a hard money loan to perform.

We backed out because there was a real possibility the city inspectors would have required us to redo the work to make the units habitable. Had we taken a hard money loan and closed the deal, we would have been on the hook to finish those repairs and ensure all work was done to code. Based on what we'd seen, we were not confident the work done *was* to code, so we left.

Another more probable case is that refinancing will take much longer than anticipated. Many banks won't finance until the property is at least 90 percent rented for three months. They'll also check the roof, venting, asphalt, and other major features. Finally, the rents will need to make sense for the finance amount. You may need to hold the property for a year or more to get it into such a condition, and meanwhile you'll continue to pay the high interest on the hard money loan.

While I'm not telling you to never take a hard money loan, I am saying that you do need to think through such an option very carefully. Fully understand what your risks are. Make sure you've calculated how long it will take to complete any work necessary to refinance, and factor in the chance that proper permitting may slow down that process.

Commercial Contracts

Moving on with your purchase, once the seller approves your LOI, the next step is the actual contract. In many states these are written by an attorney and are reviewed by attorneys on both sides. Your agent may ask you to draft the contract through your lawyer, but most *can* use form contracts if you ask.

In my experience, commercial purchase-and-sale contracts tend to be more to the point than residential ones. The assumption is that both parties are experienced in this kind of transaction. It should clearly stipulate the price, earnest money and under what circumstances it's refundable, the length of time for due diligence, how long the buyer has to close, and options the buyer has for extending the closing.

Note that due diligence, which I'll cover in depth in the next chapter, encompasses *everything* related to what you need to know to purchase the property. You'll have a limited amount of time to cover all this work and, once satisfied, you'll move to closing.

After due diligence is satisfied, you'll need to get your finances in order, obtain an appraisal, and close on the deal. Of course, you should have been working closely with your lender even before the due diligence was complete, but now you'll need to move quickly. Do not underestimate the amount of paperwork you'll need to fill out, especially for some commercial loans.

The Contract

In general, when purchasing commercial properties, you're looking at sixty days from the seller's acceptance of the contract to closing. Understand that in commercial contracts, time starts when the seller signs the *contract*, not the LOI. In residential, there is no LOI, so the seller signs the contract and the clock starts ticking.

In reality, if you're obtaining an agency loan (a loan that meets Freddie Mac's and/or Fannie Mae's guidelines), closing can take ninety days. During periods when the market is extremely busy, some vendors, such as appraisers and surveyors, may take forty-five days to get to the property, which can obviously delay your closing. That's one reason you'll want to get things moving with your lender as soon as possible.

Be diligent about your timelines, especially if doing a 1031 exchange (covered in Chapter 17). In that case, time is of the essence, and if closing is delayed you could be liable for hundreds of thousands of dollars in taxes.

Finding a property that works for your model and getting it under contract are both exciting and fun. They're also the least stressful part of the process. It's now time to get our hands dirtier during due diligence.

Chapter 10
Due Diligence

IN REAL ESTATE parlance, due diligence is a nice way of saying "figure your stuff out." Within this time frame, you're expected to evaluate every aspect of the property that matters to you. Imagine having a team of inspectors ready to examine everything, primed to race when you pull a pistol's trigger.

That will happen the moment both parties sign off on the contract. If there's a debate about any part, then the guy with the starter pistol waits around until all parties sign it. Now the pistol has been fired and it's time to run. Let's see what you should examine.

The Inspection

The most obvious part of due diligence, and equally important for residential purchases, is the inspection. Being a crucial part of the property acquisition process, this is where many contracts go off their rails. Things get emotional. You get emotional. You cry. You swear. Most of the time, no one dies.

Really, you'll need to take a deep breath. Stop and do that. Yes. I mean it. Take a deep breath. An inspection is not the place or time to stress. First, you need to understand why you're doing the inspection.

The answer will depend on a variety of factors such as the current market and price negotiations that happened prior to the contract being signed. If this is a hot property, or you got it for a hot price, your inspection may be informational only. In other words, you can only buy the property or back out of the contract. There's no in-between.

Similarly, in the commercial world there's a fair assumption that you're not going to hand over a list telling the seller to replace some doorknobs and a closet door. Those are all trivial wear-and-tear items and you should assume you'll take care of a fair share of them during the first few months of ownership. For some reason, every time we take possession of a building, the tenants suddenly remember all the things wrong in their units from the past ten years. It might be that we're the first owners who care enough to listen to them.

You're not going to get a price reduction for something that was obvious when you placed an offer. For example, don't ask them for credit on exterior paint. The state of the exterior was completely evident before you put in your offer. If you really feel the building cannot proceed without paint, then adjust your price in the LOI for the cost.

What *should* you look for in an inspection? You're really after the major components of the building: plumbing, electrical, foundation, roof, the attic, and the crawlspace. These are also not obvious during a walkthrough but are all items that can destroy your ROI if they're severe enough.

I remember one out-of-state property where I flew in for the inspection, but Joe had to stay home. When he called to ask what I thought, this was our conversation.

Me: Stopped at the police station. They said it's the usual, drug dealers and prostitutes. Chatted with their property manager. Most of the tenants aren't paying. There's garbage everywhere. The windows are all boarded. Some units are uninhabitable. Dated.

Joe: (pause) So not much is wrong with it?

Me: No. Nothing we can't handle.

On another day, at a different property, we found that many of the support beams in the crawl space needed to be replaced, or at some point the building would collapse. That would have been bad. Did we buy the building? Yes, we did, but in that case, we negotiated a price reduction because the fix was expensive and the problem was previously unknown. We also had a great contractor who specialized in foundation issues and structural engineering and were confident we could tackle it.

Meeting the Tenants

Should you inspect every unit? Yes and no. I make a point of personally *entering* every unit in order to uncover potential issues, occasionally have chats with the tenants, and verify that the property is what the seller claimed it to be. In one case, we found the units were significantly smaller than represented. The seller claimed the property had one-bedroom units, but they turned out to be studios. During an inspection you're looking for general problems, and not so much for specific ones, though a unit down to the studs should stand out.

Chatting with your future tenants is also worthwhile. This isn't as much for the inspection as for your knowledge. What demographics rent in your building? What do they like about the neighborhood and what don't they like? Do they enjoy living there? Always be friendly and never bring up any issues such as non-payment of rent. Remember, this isn't your building yet.

Occasionally, you can discover building issues through tenants but keep in mind that they might not be truthful. Always have your inspector verify anything of significant cost. Sometimes, too, you can uncover who your primary competitors are. During one inspection, a tenant made a point of explaining that the property across the street had larger units for less money. I verified his claim was true, and we bought that building too.

Detailed Inspections

Should you also inspect every appliance and switch? For residential buildings, this is probably worthwhile because a faulty refrigerator or range can affect your bottom line significantly. In larger buildings, you really don't want to do that. First, an inspection with that level of detail will cost you a fortune. Second, the tenants will let you know if things are broken. In my experience, they're more than happy to point these faults out. Finally, you're not likely to get any credit on the property price for these repairs unless literally half the appliances need to be replaced.

Should you do a survey, environmental study, or sewer scope? Some of these, especially a survey, may be required by the lender. Environmental and seismic studies should be carried out only if required, as they're typically expensive. If your multifamily property is next door to a gas station or has a river in the backyard, the bank may require an environmental study. Similarly, if your property is in California near a major fault line, they may ask for a seismic evaluation. For these studies, always ascertain the costs up front. Never write anyone a blank check.

Negotiating After the Inspection

When it comes to negotiating, try to keep your cool. These discussions can become very heated and often at some point one or both parties will emotionally dig a trench and hunker down. The thing is, these negotiations are rarely even sided. One party usually has the better cards. If you're in a hot market, understand that the seller can easily find another buyer, so he won't be overly motivated to take a lot off the price. If your asks are modest, a seller may concede to some of your requests rather than taking the risk that you'll walk away —unless of course the market is extremely hot and another offer higher than yours is waiting as backup.

The following questions may help you decide what to ask for.

Was the issue already disclosed, either visually or verbally/in writing prior to the contract?

If this issue isn't rectified, will the building not be operational?

Based on the costs of the repairs, what will your ROI be if you pay for them?

How does the price you negotiated compare to other properties on the market?

How much will the repairs *really* cost?

Are you fine walking away if the seller doesn't accept your requests?

The last question is key. Don't walk away from a property that will still make you good money. However, if the issues weren't disclosed prior to the contract being signed and the resulting costs will now destroy your ROI, you should feel comfortable with walking. Some sellers *will* bend if they know you'll truly do that.

In truth, inspections are useful tools and usually the least of your problems. In the commercial world, they're more for buy/no buy decisions. The bulk of the findings are informative only. For example, we have our inspectors look for safety hazards. These repairs are too small to bug the sellers, but by fixing them ourselves we may save a future lawsuit or two.

Examining the Finances

In contrast to physical inspections, the financial inspections can be trickier. In my experience, it's rare that perfectly functioning buildings are listed for sale. More often, they were mismanaged, or not managed at all.

Chapter 10

The first thing you'll want to do is examine the leases. How many are month-to-month instead of yearly? Be especially careful of last-minute two-year leases at low rates. For both residential and commercial purchases, the contract should stipulate that the buyers must approve all new leases. This practice is less common in commercial buildings, but you should keep an eye on it. The length of your leases will determine how long it will take to turn a struggling building around, since you cannot raise a unit's rent until the occupant's lease is finished.

Because you're going into the units anyway, now is a good time to calculate how much you'll need to spend to remodel each unit, and how much rent you can then charge. For this reason, I have my general contractor with me at the inspection. Sometimes I don't even have an inspector, since a contractor can also identify many major issues with a property.

As part of verifying what rents you can charge, be sure to check whether your building is part of a low-income housing plan. Don't be dissuaded if it is; I've found cases where they're very generous to the landlord in the allowed rents. Do verify how high you can go. In theory, the seller should always disclose housing plans well before the LOI, but this doesn't always happen. As a rule, never depend on the seller to provide crucial information necessary for you to run the building. That's part of due diligence.

Even if your building is in a rent-control plan, it may be possible to exit it. This usually takes several years with phased notices to tenants and raised rents, but it can be a relatively easy value-add, since rent-limited buildings often sell for much less per door.

Another item you'll want to review closely is the expenses, especially for maintenance. I've seen ridiculously high maintenance costs on many properties, and this is one key area where you can dramatically improve the ROI.

Does the current property manager spend a lot on advertising vacant units? You typically don't need this, since there are many free or reasonably priced online options to market rentals.

Make sure to review the utility costs as previously detailed. Water costs vary dramatically even between towns, but the usage should be similar. If it's not, you probably have one or more leaks. Make sure your inspector looks for water leaks. Depending on how accessible the leak locations are, the repair could be costly. You may also be able to reduce water costs by installing water-saving shower nozzles and new toilets. Nowadays they cost the same as the less efficient ones.

In terms of insurance, don't assume that the rate will be the same as what the seller pays. Make sure to get some quotes. Some companies won't insure a building older than a certain year, while others won't insure buildings with some types of foundations and siding. You don't want to learn these things at the last minute. You also don't want to find out that your insurance company is doubling its rates in that area. Using global warming as an excuse, many insurers are doing exactly that, especially in coastal areas.

Regarding property taxes, unless you live in a state where taxes are recalculated at sale, such as California, you can usually expect to pay a similar amount as the seller.

Making the Call

Finally, when your due diligence is complete, you'll need to make a call on whether to step up and close the deal or back out of the contract. You should never make this decision on a whim. The most glaring example of when you should back out is when the property no longer follows your model because during the due diligence you uncovered something that so dramatically changed the ROI that the building no longer makes financial sense.

For example, I once backed out of a building because it was surrounded by burned out homes and dilapidated shacks. I had been led to believe this was a transitioning neighborhood, but found no evidence for that when I flew out to inspect it. Since the neighborhood profile was part of our model, it was an easy decision.

If you do discover an unseen defect for which the repair expense will make the building undesirable, consider asking the seller for a price reduction. In such a case, you have little to lose, since you're prepared to walk anyway. If the issue is severe enough, the seller will realize that other buyers will bring up the same issue so their best bet may be to just work with you. Be reasonable with your requests and you may be surprised.

My hope is that you will like the building because you have to actually *close* on real estate to begin making money. You're almost to the fun part, but first you have a major hill. No other part of the process brings me to my knees and sucks the energy out of me as much as dealing with the banks. So go get a drink and let's begin.

Chapter 11
Working with Banks

BANKS CAN BE incredibly difficult to deal with. Seriously, why can't they just hand out blank checks to everyone who wants them, and just accept their word that the loan will be paid back? Unfortunately, we don't live in such a world so we need to answer their questions and fit into one of the myriad programs they offer.

Mortgage Brokers

Navigating these programs can be a nightmare and I therefore cannot recommend more strongly that you choose a mortgage *broker* instead of working with the bank yourself. Like many things in real estate, there are exceptions to this—let's say you have an excellent preexisting relationship with your bank and they offer a program that fits you well. But in most cases, a broker will offer far more flexibility.

The problem with dealing with only one bank is it limits what loans you can access. Different banks offer vastly different programs. Each transaction is different and where one bank's program works terrifically for one investor, it won't apply to another. Therefore, you need a broker with access to many banks. For a commercial loan, pick a broker with very close ties to Freddie Mac and Fannie Mae partners, as those are easily the two biggest players on the market.

Obtaining a good mortgage broker can be challenging. These are busy people, and they're inundated with jokers even more than agents are. Don't be surprised to be interviewed when you first talk with one, as they're more suspicious of you than you are of them. Nevertheless, you can break a lot of ice by obtaining a recommendation from your agent. With that in hand, the broker will trust you more. Remember how I earlier recommended obtaining an agent recommendation from the lender? Yeah. If you're starting out, try getting a recommendation from both sides until you have success.

This book will help you with that first discussion with the lender. He's first going to ask about your resources, then about what types of properties you're looking for. You may have a particular property in mind, but if you don't, this is a perfect chance to utilize your model. Based on that, the broker may mention some programs that could potentially fit you.

Much like dealing with an agent, you can tell that a broker knows what he's doing by how he talks and acts. Most aren't into the fluff. You tell him what you want to finance and he tells you if you're smoking crack, and if you're not then he'll list some various programs that might fit your needs. You can then have a rough idea of your down payment and interest rate, though keep in mind these *will* change once the bank examines the numbers and your experience or if interest rates change.

Improving Your Credit

Now some of you may be starting to blush. You have bad credit and are starting to worry. If that's the case, a real estate loan may not be in your immediate plans, but it's not too difficult to change that. The simple solution to poor credit is to get a credit card. Each month, max out that card as far as you can financially afford to and at the end of the month *pay it off*. Yes, the whole thing. That's the important part. If you keep doing this, you'll notice your credit rating shoot up faster than your blood pressure at a fast-food joint.

Chapter Disclaimer

I'm going to be honest here. The only loans I've received have been residential and commercial loans for apartment buildings. I've never purchased a hotel, strip mall, restaurant, office building, airport, or amusement park. Each of these may require radically different loans from what I describe here. For example, lenders will want to review tenant leases in retail establishments and office buildings. If you buy a chicken farm, they may want cease-and-desist letters sent to all wolves. I really don't know about those loans, but I do have a lot of experience with apartment buildings, so I'll stick to them in this chapter.

Differences Between Residential and Commercial Loans

Now it's time to discuss the differences between residential and commercial loans. For residential, loans are similar to those for buying a house. The bank looks at how much you make. They *do* factor in the rents, but they'll ultimately check whether *you* can afford this property. If you have other properties that are profitable, they'll strengthen your case by providing extra income to your balance sheet, but they'll also hurt because the bank will worry that you might be too deeply leveraged.

In a commercial loan, you're buying a business. The bank is therefore going to verify that it's profitable. If it's not, for example if all the units are vacant, there are options such as hard money. One condition is always crucial for commercial loans: Banks need to see that you have experience.

Loan	Experience Necessary?	Loan Size	Interest Rates	Typical Term	Typical Amortization	Closing Costs
Hard Money	No, but varies by lender	Usually small	The highest	under a year	1 point per month	Usually 2 points
Bridge	Depends on product loan will be rolled into	Can be large	High	1-2 years	25 years	Extremely high
Residential	No	Small	Low	30 years	30 years	Low
Commercial – local bank	Yes	Medium	Low-Medium	10 years	25 years	Medium
Commercial – Fannie/Freddie(non recourse)	Yes	Large	Very Low - Low	10 years	25 years	Medium

Gaining Experience

It doesn't matter who you are. No bank is going to give a loan for a forty-unit multifamily building unless the buyer can prove she knows what she's doing. Without that experience, you'll be rejected quicker than you ever were in high school. There are three ways around this.

The first is to start small and gain experience. That's what we did. We started with a duplex, which is residential. Later, we bought a fourplex and triplex, which are also residential. Our first commercial loan was a thirteen-unit apartment building. The bank worked with us because we already owned seven units (we had sold the duplex at that point), and thirteen wasn't that much more than seven, from their point of view.

Our next building had twenty-four units. We already owned twenty, one of which was a commercial building, so the bank was fine. As we added buildings, we followed the same pattern. If the number of units in the new building isn't vastly more than what you own now, the bank will accept your experience.

What if you're in a hurry and want to get into the bigger stuff now? In that case, you'll need to partner. I'll cover that more in the next chapter on partners. I'll just say now that when considering a partner, you need to bring something to the table for that to happen. Real estate loans require two things: experience and money. If you don't have the experience, you'll have to make it up in money. I've actually had someone ask me to go fifty-fifty on a building, where I'm putting up the money and experience, *and* managing it. May I just say that drugs are bad for you?

The third option is to put enough down for the bank to not care about your lack of experience. This will need to be at least forty percent, and maybe more. Keep in mind that your ROI will suck, but if you have the funds and want admittance, this is a quick way to accomplish that. Recognize that there's a *reason* banks look for experience. When you take possession of that large multifamily, you'll be jumping directly into the fire. Make sure you're ready.

Commercial loans take longer to process than residential loans. While sixty days is common, nonrecourse loans (explained soon) will take longer. Make sure to factor this into your closing date on the contract.

Differences Between Loans

Now that I've explained how to find a broker for a loan, it's time to discuss what makes various loan packages different. There is a dizzying array of them and mortgage brokers seem to take glee in rolling them past you. The following will help you evaluate them.

Recourse vs. nonrecourse – This states whether, in case of default, the bank can go after you personally if it doesn't obtain enough from the seizure of the property to cover the loan. In other words, if you fail fantastically, can the bank take your own home and possessions? Most loans are recourse, meaning banks *can* go after you, but if you know what you're doing, you shouldn't worry about that.

If you buy with a decent ROI, your building will continue to make money even with some vacancies. As time goes on, rents are likely to increase, and you'll be able to withstand even severe circumstances. Finally, even if you somehow fail completely, you've hopefully purchased in an area with lots of jobs and low housing availability, so the bank should get enough from selling your seized property to cover the loan.

I can understand that the prospect is daunting, so banks do offer nonrecourse options. These loans are tougher to obtain and take longer to process because the bank will obviously want to ensure that their cash is in good hands.

Term – This is the duration of the loan. It is *not* the amortization, meaning how long it would take to completely pay off the property. In residential loans, the term and amortization are often the same, but in commercial loans they're usually different. When the term expires, you will *need to obtain a new loan*. Understand that this means a whole new application, appraisal, and the associated loan costs. In the commercial world, ten years is a normal term, but twenty-five and thirty-year terms exist.

Amortization – This is how long it will take to pay off the loan, assuming the term extends that far. Note that when you're calculating your mortgage payment, this is the number to use – not the term. While thirty-year amortization (and even longer) is common in residential, it's not as common in commercial. Twenty-five years is the standard, but sometimes an appraiser might call out that the building only has twenty years of life, and the bank may shorten the amortization period and thus increase your monthly payments. If this happens, keep in mind that appraisers' judgments can be overruled with common-sense arguments, and different banks are more or less willing to reconsider.

Some loans change their amortization period during the term. For example, they may start with five years of interest only, then switch to a thirty-year amortization afterwards.

Prepayment penalties – This is often a surprise for those coming from residential loans where prepayment penalties are less common, but they are common in commercial. Before entering a loan agreement, make sure you understand what those penalties are, and balance them against your plans for the property.

Yield maintenance is the most common prepayment penalty for *nonrecourse loans*. It can also be the costliest. It's best illustrated with an example. Imagine that you've financed a one-million-dollar loan at five percent with a term of ten years. For simplicity, we'll pretend that the loan is interest-only, even though ten-year interest-only loans are currently rare. The payments on this loan will be $50,000 per year.

Two years later, you decide to sell the building. You think this is a no-brainer because it has now appreciated by five hundred thousand dollars. You plan to take that money, plus your original down payment, and buy a much larger building. You're thrilled that interest rates have now plunged to three percent, so your ROI on the new building will be better. But you didn't factor in the prepayment penalty. How much will you owe for yield maintenance?

Yield maintenance protects the bank from this situation. If the interest rates go down, you'll owe the bank what it would have made for the duration of the loan.

In this case, the interest rates went down from five to three percent, so the difference is two percent. You have eight years remaining on the loan, so you'll owe

$$.8 \times (\text{yearly interest at } 5\% - \text{yearly interest at } 3\%) = 8 \times (50{,}000 - 30{,}000) = 160{,}000$$

Yup. Of your $500,000 profit, $160,000 would go to the bank

Of course, if interest rates go up, then the yield maintenance is zero. For a real life example, on one building we purchased from a syndicate, this bit them hard. The sellers even tried to delay closing in hopes of a better interest rate, but any gains would have been erased by our lawyers.

Therefore, it would be very foolish to choose a yield maintenance loan if you're hoping to flip the building in a year or two.

In most *recourse loans*, the typical prepayment penalty is stepdown. This is simple to calculate. After one year, the penalty is a certain percentage of the loan (say 3 percent). After two years, that again goes down a percent, and with each year it goes down another percent until it reaches zero. The advantage of this type of penalty is you know exactly when you can refinance. It also rarely produces as ghastly a penalty as yield maintenance.

Fees – These will be specified on the lender LOI, and you should pay special attention to them. Beware specifically of those that are open-ended. Legal fees, especially on bridge loans, can border on predatory. Get an estimate from the lender on what those fees should be, and be prepared to question sharply if the end amount differs significantly from that estimate. We once questioned an extraordinary legal fee, and then received an itemized list of expenses. The only problem was it mentioned conversations with us that never took place. In some cases, we weren't even in the country on those dates. You can imagine there was a heated discussion concerning this, and a refund.

The list of fees will include standard ones like appraisal, but also nonstandard ones such as environmental and seismic. You can ignore these when they obviously do not apply. For example, if seismic activity is rare in the region, the lender shouldn't require that inspection. On the other hand, if there's a river in your backyard, a swamp in your front yard, three eagle nests on the premises, and an ivory-billed woodpecker was reported last week on your property, there will probably be an environmental inspection. These items will typically mention "subject to PCA (Property Condition Assessment)" on the LOI, indicating they'll only apply if the appraisal calls for them.

Holdbacks – These can be frustrating for the borrower but are there to protect the lender's interests. They are funds you deposit at closing for specific purposes. There are two primary types.

The first, and most common, is for work necessary to bring the building up to standards. The goal is to motivate you to complete work the lender feels is necessary for the building to meet its financial goals. Of course, if you're low on cash, holdbacks make the project more difficult because you must first pay for the work, provide evidence of its completion to the bank, and then apply for your money back.

Pay close attention to whether the bank has fees for returning your money back to you after the repairs. I've seen LOIs stating that the borrower must pay $5,000 per withdrawal, but this of course was in the fine print. Make sure to read *everything*.

The second type of holdback is what I'll term "situational." They're special cases when the lender believes there are circumstances that may prevent tenants from paying. During Covid, lenders often required a year or more of mortgage payments as a holdback. Note that borrowers were still required to make regular loan payments during this time. They couldn't rely on the money held by the bank, which according to the contracts would be returned in eighteen months to two years if the building was in good financial order.

These holdbacks are of no benefit to you but serve as insurance for the bank against your failure to make the necessary repairs, or your tenants' failures to pay the rent. On your part, they just increase the amount of capital you must invest in the property, though I typically don't include them in the ROI because they are eventually returned.

Make sure to understand how long you need to wait to reclaim holdback funds. Also, check for withdrawal fees, as mentioned above. This is your precious cash, after all, that they're tying up. Finally, understand that estimates for repairs, and the necessity of such repairs, is negotiable. Numerous times we've had our contractors find more cost-effective solutions and reduced the required holdbacks.

> **Replacement funds** – These are related to holdbacks but are paid monthly instead of at closing. The way they work is this: The bank runs your property through a little computer that calculates the number of refrigerators, stoves, air conditioners, flooring, furnaces, caulking, and garden gnomes that will break each year.

The computer will then estimate the cost of each item and how many will break each year of the loan. For example, on a recent financing the computer decided that we would need 75,400 stripes of caulk at a price of ten cents each over ten years. Based on what it predicts will break, it sums that amount for the year. You pay that monthly.

The bank does this because they're concerned that you might not repair the property, so if you don't, they have some funds to get it to working shape. While holdbacks are typically for big ticket items, replacement funds are for the wear-and-tear stuff.

As with holdbacks, make sure you read the fine print. Banks usually charge loan maintenance and setup fees. After all, you wouldn't expect the bank to take your money and give it back to you for free, right? To receive your money back, you'll typically have to provide contractor receipts detailing the work provided, which must match the repairs specified for that year (you can't replace all refrigerators at once). The bank may or may not charge you to send an inspector to verify it.

Assumable loans – When selling a property, if your loan has high interest rates and a yield maintenance prepayment penalty, you may want to ask buyers to assume your loan. This means the bank replaces your names with the buyers' names on the loan.

Many loans are assumable, though there's typically a fee of around one percent for the transfer. If current interest rates are much lower than the interest on your loan, however, don't assume the buyer will want to do this, as assuming your higher interest rates will increase their mortgage payments and lower their ROI.

Bank relationship – Some banks will require you to deposit some amount in their bank to form a "relationship." This amount is typically between $50,000 and $100,000. Doing so usually will get you a better interest rate on loans, but some banks simply won't give you the loan without it. The rules for what you do with those funds vary. In some cases, you can pull it out immediately after the property finances. In others, you can use those funds for the down payment. Other banks require that you maintain a minimum balance. Make sure you understand those restrictions before accepting the loan. Also, if there's a minimum balance required over the duration of the loan, you'll need to factor those "lost" funds into your ROI by adding them to your down payment.

Chapter 11

Bridge Loans

When looking at a value-add property (explained later), it may sometimes be in such poor condition that traditional financing isn't possible. In another example, the property may not satisfy the bank requirements for a nonrecourse loan. I've already covered one option available in this case: the hard money loan. Here, I'll discuss a more reasonable alternative: the bridge loan.

Bridge loans are just that—a bridge to another loan. They typically last one or two years and allow you to get the building stabilized and ready for a refinance. If you do your job well, they may also provide a means to pull your down payment out on the refinance. Bridge loans can be useful tools, but you need to take care.

In our experience, lenders for these types of loans can be even more predatory than hard money loans. They are notorious for high legal fees, and I've even seen one change terms on the contract from the LOI with the hope the borrowers didn't notice. You'll need to pay extra attention for these types of loans.

Typically, interest rates for bridge loans are higher than conventional loans, and lenders may charge one or two points at the end of the loan if you don't refinance with them. They also have specific requirements on what you must do to the building. This is necessary because the lender intends to sell your loan to another servicer or will transfer it to Freddie Mac/Fannie Mae, and they need to ensure your building meets the new party's requirements.

Personally, I find that bridge loans can be a useful tool for purchasing properties that won't finance otherwise, but they should be used as a last resort. The extra fees can easily add four to five percent to the purchase price and they can be among the worst banks to deal with in terms of paperwork, withdrawing holdbacks, bureaucracy, and fraud.

Cash-Out Refinances

Cash-out refinances have been made famous by the BRRRR (Buy, Rehab, Rent, Refinance, Repeat) method, which is a common buzzword for purchasing a value-add property, stabilizing it, then pulling your down payment out in a refinance. Note that pretty much no one who makes their income off investments (as compared to overpriced training courses on investments) calls it that. Investors have been using this strategy since long before the buzzword was invented. Back then it was bundled into… "common sense."

This is a great strategy, but if you intend to use it, make sure to plan ahead. As mentioned earlier, a prepayment penalty can put a wrench into those plans, though some loans offer provisions for a "supplemental." This is an additional loan on top of your primary one, typically with the same bank, that allows you to regain that down payment and sometimes extra principal.

When used effectively, cash-out refinances allow you to buy something for nothing down. Keep in mind, though, that most cash-out refinance loans require you to hold the property for at least twelve months.

Another snafu that could affect your plans is rising interest rates, which may allow you to regain your original cash but lock you into a new loan at higher interest rate. Always calculate what you are paying to retrieve that money, as you may not find the effort worth it.

Paperwork

If, like me, you dreaded doing your homework in high school, you're going to absolutely hate the amount of paperwork necessary to obtain a loan. If you're applying for a nonrecourse loan, expect triple the paperwork. If you wrote a life history for yourself, it would probably be shorter than the information they need. The following are some specifics.

Chapter 11

Business Plans – Yes, you may have had to do these in high school for an imaginary business, but this is the real deal. Many banks will require one-, five-, and ten-year business plans. In your one-year plan, you're going to detail:

- What improvements you plan to make to the building
- How you intend to pay for those improvements
- What you hope to achieve in rents
- Your market justification for those rents
- How you will fill any vacancies
- Given the current leases, what percentage of them can be raised within the year?
- How you will work with any government regulations concerning rent increases
- Your estimated expenses for that year
- Your predicted profits for the year
- How your plan for this building compares to what you've already accomplished in other buildings

In your five- and ten-year plans, you'll add the following.

- Your predictions for rent increases year to year (so get your crystal ball out)
- Your corresponding predictions for increases to taxes, insurance, and other expenses
- Major improvements you intend to undertake during that time
- Your predicted profit for each year, which should grow

These are not the hundred-page business plans necessary for venture capital, but they are typically several pages long. They will be detailed, but not overly so. Remember that the bank may question anything you write, so be concise.

T-12 (Trailing 12) - This document presents the rents for the last year. In some cases, banks may also go off the T-1 (one month) or the T-3 (average of the last three months). They'll use the T-12 to verify that you will be making a profit after paying expenses and the mortgage. They'll use the T-1 or T-3 to verify that the property is currently in good shape. For example, if half the tenants suddenly leave, then the T-1 won't look so great, and the bank may not finance the property. As a rule, banks expect the building to be 90 percent occupied for the last ninety days (we call it "ninety for ninety").

Profit and loss statement - This clarifies whether the building is currently generating a profit based on the information provided by the seller. Some banks will even request the Schedule E from the seller in order to verify that the numbers reported are true. Many times, this is where things can turn tricky. There are two ways, concerning profit and loss, that the bank may choose to finance the building.

First, they may choose to finance the building in as-is condition, meaning they just take the current rents and condition of the building. This is fine for Class A and B properties, but not always for C.

The alternative is to use pro forma numbers. If this is the case, you'll need a well-written business plan that details the costs necessary to turn the building, and what you believe future rents will be. For pro forma finance to work, you need to have a relationship with the bank because you're asking them to trust you. They're going to want to see your experience. I've already detailed at the beginning of this chapter how to achieve it.

Business debt schedule – There are numerous online sites that show you how to create this, and some software that can do it for you. The debt schedule shows expected expenses per month

Chapter 11

as balanced by income. The goal is to show the bank that you won't run out of money.

Resume – Yes, you're applying for a job. You're asking to be the CEO of Your Real Estate Holdings, so the bank will want to see your qualifications. Your resume should detail what similar projects you've undertaken and your successes. It should read much like an employment resume, but instead of companies, you'll list projects. For each project, you should state

- How much you paid
- The number of units and their makeup (1BR 1BA, 2 BR 1BA, etc.)
- The property's location
- What you did to the property
- The gain in rents while you owned it (or since you've owned it)
- How long you (have) owned it
- If you sold the property, the selling price

You're essentially *showing* the bank that you have the experience necessary for this project and therefore their money is in good hands.

What if you don't *have* the experience? Should you fake it? No. The banks will catch on quickly, you'll be the fool, and you'll burn more than a few bridges. If you don't have the experience, then either go get it beforehand or find an experienced partner if you can provide the funds. Note that residential loans (four or less units) won't ask for a resume.

Schedule of real estate owned – This is a list of all the real estate you *currently* own. It does not include those you have sold. For each building, provide the following.

- How much you paid

- Address of the property
- How much it's worth now
- When you bought it
- How much you owe
- The monthly payment
- Which LLC owns it

LLC incorporation documents – While you should always consult a CPA or attorney experienced in real estate, in most cases you'll want your buildings in an LLC. Often, each property will be in its own entity. You'll need to send the bank your LLC articles of incorporation documents. In some cases, the bank may require modifications to your structure and bylaws. Your CPA or attorney will be able to assist you with that.

W2s and personal financial statements – I'm assuming you've submitted these for other purposes before.

Property manager information – I've had banks interview my property manager. See Chapter 14 for details on selecting one.

Eldest child's favorite color and blood type – It often baffles me what banks need. I've been asked how many students and military personnel live in the building and the top five employers for the tenants. For the students, I had to provide the colleges and universities they attend. I swear, one of these days they'll ask for my kids' blood types.

For a recent refinance, I received fifty pages of forms to fill out. This was a modest amount, since no resume or business plan is necessary for a refinance. If you need to enter a quiet room to scream, I'll wait.

Now that you've vented, just take a deep breath and start your homework. Remember that it's perfectly fine to ask your broker for clarifications or perform an online search.

Chapter 11

With the loan behind us, it's time to take a step back and examine more details of the transaction before we proceed to closing in Chapter 17. Up first is working with partners.

Chapter 12
Working with Partners

THE AREA WE were currently investing in had so many buildings with killer ROIs that we'd sold everything we had in Washington state and used all our funds on buildings in our new target area. One day we found ourselves with an unexpected problem: we'd already spent every spare penny on real estate when the unthinkable happened. A building I'd had my eye on for some time came onto the market. I'd thought for sure the owners would want the sky, but they didn't. This building had the best numbers I'd seen, and I wanted it badly.

Not only were the numbers great, but it was on the same street as several of our other buildings, and until then it had served as competition. This was the ultimate buy. Not only would we pick up a building with amazing numbers, but we'd also build "synergy" with our other properties. The new building even had a leasing/management office. It was perfect, but we didn't have enough money.

Chapter 12

Partnership As a Solution

I mentioned the building to someone who had expressed interest in out-of-state investments. He was very interested, had the funds, but lacked the experience. Both of us realized the only way to make this happen was to partner up. It was easily the scariest decision I'd made in real estate. Why? Because I dissolve partnerships daily and sell their buildings, I'm very aware how fragile they are.

When I brought up the subject with Joe, he was beyond nervous. We'd always purchased things ourselves. We have a good formula going, even if it requires painful decisions at times. How would a majority partner work with us? Because he was bringing most of the funds, he wanted veto power, which was certainly a reasonable request. Would his goals align with ours?

This was in the middle of Covid, so I arranged for a Zoom call between Joe, myself, him, and his wife. Every decision maker had to be there. After a lengthy discussion, the topics of which I'll discuss later, we agreed to pursue the building.

That decision turned out well for all parties. The following illustrates a much different process.

Investigating Syndicates

Several people had been pestering me for some time to invest with them. Unlike our partner above, they weren't interested in the details of investing. They simply wanted to hand their money over and watch it grow. The financial form of that is called a syndicate.

Imagine you want to buy a fifty million dollar building but you only have a dollar twenty-five. The bank is unlikely to give you that loan. However, if you can convince fifteen people to give you a million dollars, then you'll have thirty percent for the down payment. Of course, *you* still want to have control over the property and you want to be paid for your work in finding, purchasing, managing, and ultimately selling that building. The mechanism to accomplish this is the syndicate. It's like a mini-stock.

Joe and I have spent a great deal of time researching syndicates. We have friends who run them, so we started by chatting with them, but we needed more details. We bought several books and devoured them. We had preliminary discussions with our lawyer, began considering legal entities and making a list of potential qualified investors, and stood before a final go/no go decision. Ultimately, we didn't move forward.

Why Partner?

Working with partners can be either easy or the most stressful thing in existence. We've purchased several buildings from partnerships that fell apart. We know people who have had nervous breakdowns from partnerships.

Let's first discuss why you would want to do this. I'll focus on partnerships for now, then syndicates. As I described in my own story, the *proper* reason to seek a partner is to purchase a building you ordinarily would have bought if you had the funds. Notice the nuance: This building checks everything in your model. It's awesome. You just don't have the funds. In that case, it's time to search for moneyed partners. The sell should be easy because there's really no sell: You yourself want it badly, and you can explain why clearly.

On the flip side, you may have the funds but not the experience. As I've already explained, banks won't give you a commercial loan if you haven't been in investment real estate long. In that case, you'll need to find someone who does have the needed experience and show them that the property you're after makes sense.

Finding Partners

The search for partners should be on a personal level. Absolutely do not place an advertisement and under no circumstances should you ever answer one. This partner should be someone with whom you've had some experience, though ideally is not related to you. Trust me on that. Both of our families have members who don't speak to each other due to financial disputes. In our experience, it's just not worth it.

While syndicates have strict rules about how you can search for partners, partnerships themselves do not. I'd advise you to stick to people who have previously expressed a desire to work with you, and who have either the funds or the experience necessary. Note that if it's the experience you require, you'll probably need to be direct and approach investors you trust about the prospect of working with each other. Don't expect them to hand you something right away. More likely, they'll remember you when something irresistible comes up.

Evaluating Partners

When the opportunity to partner arises, you'll need to sit down and have a tough discussion with them. This is *not* an interview! Instead, you'll discuss whether your views are the same regarding the following:

- Are you both interested in flipping or buy and hold?
- What types of buildings are you seeking? Are you most comfortable with class B or class C? How large of a building do you want?
- Is appreciation or cash flow more important?

There are no right or wrong answers here. You both need to know whether you're on the same page. The absolutely last thing you want is for one partner to want to sell when the other does not. Besides ensuring that you share the same investing goals, the following are also important:

- Both parties need to be easygoing. There *will* be hiccups along the way, sometimes big ones, and this is not a time for high anxiety.
- You should get along. Keep in mind that you need to be business partners, not best friends. You will be "married" for the next several years, so be aware of that.
- Assess the long-term stability of the other party. This is a tricky one, since personal questions are unlikely to receive a cheerful response. However, a divorce could cause major issues for your partnership and may force a sale of the property against everyone's wishes. So if one party gets up during a meeting and dumps a bowl of spaghetti on the other, you may want to rethink this partnership.
- Make sure both you and your potential partner agree on timelines. When do you plan to sell the property, if at all? Are you in alignment on how long it will take to reach the target numbers? Note that two years is the norm. A lot of partnerships fall apart when one party becomes frustrated that the property continues to not perform, or they are simply not on the same page regarding goals.

Make sure to meet with *every* decision-maker in the household. In my experience, the quiet spouses are rarely so behind closed doors. Like my grandma always said: It's the quiet one you want to be scared of. Ensure *everyone* involved agrees.

The Partnership Agreement

The next step will be to bring in an attorney to draft the partnership rules in writing. This is also the time to discuss tough things like ownership percentage and decision making. Personally, I feel that the party bringing the majority of funds should have legal override power. In other words, she should be able to dictate actions if there's a disagreement. Understand, of course, that executing such power will be a hostile action, but this is a good legal protection for your money.

At a high level, the legal agreement should spell out the following.

- Who is bringing what percentage of the initial funds?
- Are there any silent partners? These are partners with no say in the operation of the business. You may find partners who prefer this, but personally I would never agree to be silent with my money on the line.
- What is the management structure? There needs to be some resolution process for when partners disagree.
- How are distributions calculated? Typically, expenses, along with a specific return on investment, are either split between both partners or are distributed to one preferred partner first, then the other. If one partner is preferred, then it is typically only up to a certain return, and afterwards all funds are split by percentage. For example, if one party (we'll call him Ralph) brings 90 percent of the funds, but the ownership is split 75/25 for Ralph/Smith, the agreement may stipulate that Ralph receives the entire distribution up to a 5 percent per annum return, and the remaining profits are split to make a 75/25 return. The reason for such a stipulation is to ensure the provider of the majority provider of funds receives priority in obtaining a return.
- If additional money is required to pay bills, how is that split?
- If one partner wishes to buy out the other partner, how is the value of the building determined and what is the procedure? Is it possible for one partner to buy out by forcing the other to sell out after some time?
- When is the earliest that the building can be placed for sale? Do both parties need to agree, or can one force the sale? Typically, both partners must agree up to a certain year. After that, either party may force a sale.

- What happens in the event of a death to one of the partners?
- How will proceeds from the sale of the property be calculated?

Perhaps the most crucial aspect of the agreement is the out: you must define what options each side has for ending the partnership and/or for forcing a sale. Understand that financial priorities change with time. You both may agree to hold the building for at least five years, but what happens after that? Typically, the agreement states that the decision to sell is revisited each year.

The next steps before a financial transaction can take place are to create an LLC and to open a bank account for the partnership. All managing partners should have access.

The partnership I mentioned at the beginning of the chapter has been very successful. The building indeed turned out to be an excellent buy and in many ways is already exceeding our expectations. Our partnership is robust: we don't sit around a campfire and tell each other secrets at night, but we have an excellent working relationship. Now, however, I must turn to a very different type of partnership that is in most ways a completely different beast: syndicates.

My Opinions on Syndicates

You can find entire books on syndicates and if you're interested in starting one, I highly recommend you buy a few. There are numerous legal nuances, and this is one area of real estate where you can go to jail for doing something you were completely unaware was illegal.

First, if you're new to real estate investing, don't even think about starting a syndicate. Syndicates are really for those with a lot of experience. Personally, I wouldn't dream of starting one with fewer than one hundred units of experience – and that does *not* include units where you aren't the primary manager. I also would never invest in someone else's syndicate who has fewer than that.

I won't beat around the bush here. I don't like syndicates. The major reason I don't like them is that the economics are completely different. I've already explained in depth how "normal" investment economics work: You buy a property and make money either from the rents or from appreciation. Based on advertisements, syndicates *appear* to work that way but they actually don't.

Syndicates are run by managers. These managers typically receive a higher percentage of the profits than their investors, but that's not all. They also make bonuses when they meet certain goals: when a project funds, when the property buy closes, and when the building is sold and funds are distributed. Let's look at how that might work.

Let's say a syndicate's goal is to fund and purchase a twenty-million-dollar apartment building. The following are typical ways the syndicate managers will be paid.

- For 30 percent down, they'll need six million from investors. When they reach that amount, the managers will receive a 1 percent bonus, or $200,000.
- The syndicate places an offer, finances, and closes on the property. The managers receive a 1 to 2 percent bonus, or another $200,000 to $400,000.
- After purchase, the syndicate manages the property. There is some minimum amount the managers earn from the rents collected, and that is usually *before* expenses. While most banks will require that loan payments be made first, the managers will receive their annuity before other required expenses, and therefore the building may actually run at a deficit while the manager is still profiting.
- After the managers have received their initial percentage from rental income, the expenses are deducted and the investors usually receive their payment from the profit due to rents. This is up to a certain percentage. After that, profits are shared with the management by percentage. For example, let's say the building makes $400,000 in profits per

year. The first $100,000 may go to the managers. After that, the next $200,000 in profits is split between the investors, and the remaining $100,000 is split fifty-fifty between the investors and syndicate managers. In this scenario the managers will receive $150,000 and the investors will split the remaining $250,000. This is a vast simplification because expenses aren't factored in and payouts are rarely this simple, but gives you an idea.

- When the building is sold later for thirty million, the managers will make two percent, or $600,000.
- The profits from the sale are divided first among the investors, usually to ensure they make a certain percentage of holding per year. After that, the profits are often divided between investors and managers.

Let's play devil's advocate and see what the managing partners make if the property underperforms.

- $200,000 from the funding bonus
- $200,000 to $400,000 as a closing bonus
- $100,000 per year

In other words, even if the building doesn't perform *at all* and is sold after one year, the syndicate managers still make $500,000 to $700,000! From this, you can see that syndicates have a major incentive to acquire and manage properties, even if their numbers aren't strong. Where they're usually bailed out is in rising property values. In a great market, buildings appreciate and it's not difficult, even after the management fees, to provide a return of 10 percent or more to investors, which is considered very good in most years and is comparable to the stock market.

Often, I've seen syndicates pick up buildings at ridiculously high numbers. For example, one syndicate picked up a complex across the street from one of mine for 20 percent more per door.

Our properties closed at the same time, and their building was condemned and required major work, while mine was a typical "floors, fixtures, and paint" value-add.

Now you may think I'm saying that all syndicates are evil, and that's not the case. Many investors have earned good money through syndicates. My main concern is that their model, where acquisitions are rewarded more than ROI, doesn't favor the investor. Only if the building appreciates are the investors rewarded. If the market stalls, things easily turn south.

Should you start a syndicate? Recall the beginning of this chapter. If there's so much money in it, why didn't I start one myself? I'll be honest with you and admit that we seriously considered it. We did the research. We even wrote a "mission statement" on how we would be the first syndicate to reward performance instead of acquisitions. We would take lower fees in favor of profits when our buildings outperformed, which we knew they would. But we still didn't move forward.

If you have dreams of sprawling homes and your own gigantic yacht, managing syndicates can be a major enabler. This is where the *real* money is made. There's no limit. However, if it were that easy, everyone would be doing it. Syndicates are *stressful*.

I have friends who run syndicates. Occasionally, one has a breakdown. It's stressful dealing with large amounts of money from high-net-worth individuals. Even silent partners are rarely silent. They have grand dreams of being wealthier themselves, and no matter what you do, they're never satisfied.

In the end, we looked at our own holdings and realized we didn't need to start a syndicate to reach our dreams of retiring early. There is such a thing as *enough* money. The well-being of our family and our sanity are a lot more important to us. We are okay with others having more money than we do.

Should *you* invest in a syndicate? In fairness, this might be an option if you determine that you can't do this yourself. However, I hope this book *has* taught you that you can do this, and that you won't enter the syndicate game. I've just heard far too many horror stories to recommend it.

If you're still interested in syndicates, read the fine print very carefully. Pay attention to what percentage ownership the managers receive compared to how much they're bringing to the table. It's not uncommon for the syndicate managers to bring nothing but take a fifty percent ownership on top of their fees. While I do believe a savvy real estate investor's skills are worth gold, this seems to me like highway robbery.

As I've already mentioned, several of my properties were purchased from failed syndicates. I've even known syndicate managers who took jobs at tech companies with the aim of directly marketing to high-net-worth individuals. My honest opinion is that you're probably better off investing in a REIT (Real Estate Investment Trust). I'm sure they have their issues, too, but their reporting is far more stringently controlled by the SEC than syndicates, who operate more like the Wild West.

In the end, partnerships—regardless of the legal entity—are one tool in an array of many available to real estate investors. Where they apply, you should use them. Do look both ways before crossing the "partner street" or you'll end up with a never-ending nightmare.

Chapter 13
Self-Managing Properties

PERSONALLY, I STRONGLY believe that every real estate investor should go through the experience of having a tenant call you at 2 a.m. because their kid flushed a toy car down the toilet, or be woken at 3 a.m. while on vacation because your tenant and his girlfriend got into a fight and she is moving out and needs to be off the lease.

Why Manage Yourself

I don't enjoy hearing about others' problems, but as a landlord they're often heaped upon me. It's part of the job, and it's a job you need to learn to do if you want to succeed. While I certainly recommend hiring a property manager at some point, you should start out by dealing directly with tenants.

It's tempting to hire a property manager immediately. Sure, they'll handle your tenants and your property, but how well? If you've never done this yourself, how will you know if they're doing a good job? You need to understand the differences between property managers, and the only proper way to do that is to start off managing your own investments.

Chapter 13

Managing a property manager is a skill that divides poor investors from great ones. This is the coliseum where gladiators spar, where investors are made, and where others falter. If you hope to survive in this world, you're going to need a system. Chaos will not work here.

Building a System

Tenant by tenant, unit by unit, you're going to build this system until you get pretty good at it. Only then will you hire a property manager, with the stipulation that they follow your system, or at least something close to it.

The key to a successful system is understanding what your tenants want. They're not looking for a best friend, but they do want someone who will care for the building. Primarily, your tenants want to just live their lives. If a toilet clogs, the heating stops working, or a cockroach crawls out and introduces itself, their lives are interrupted. Your job will be to get them back on track.

In exchange, they'll pay their rent. Just like they just want their appliances to work, you just want to keep receiving rent. Neither of you should concern yourselves much with the other's life. When tenants stop paying, you'll need to step in and fix things, but in a much different way.

Your most important resource for fixing things that break will be contractors. I'll cover them in more depth in Chapter 19, but these are the top people you need in your corner. When things fall apart—and they will—you'll need them ready and willing to fix them for a reasonable price. Identify plumbers, electricians, pest control contractors, and handymen *before* you need them. Don't wait for something to go wrong to ask for references.

My System

When I have a vacancy, I schedule an appointment with every interested tenant to see the unit on a weekend. There are numerous reasons for this, but the primary one is that I have a day job and can't be there on a moment's notice. Also, prospective tenants can be flakes. Roughly half of those who make an appointment never show up, so if I have ten people scheduled on a weekend I can expect to meet with five.

In a pinch, I'll pay a small amount to another tenant to show units, but that's only when conflicts prevent me from going to the property. Truthfully, that tenant really doesn't care about the building or my interests. I have qualifications for all tenants that are mainly financial. By allowing someone else to make decisions I may also open myself up to accusations of profiling, which these days can bring costly legal trouble. In addition, when I show the units myself, I'll become keenly aware if there's an issue preventing renters from taking it. Most potential renters are all too willing to point out why they're not interested. If it's something fixable, I can address it, but only if I know about it.

When I arrive, I bring pre-printed rental applications. Those who show up can fill one out right there or email it to me later. Within twenty-four hours I can qualify those applications and the best one will be run through an online background check. When tenants call, they ask what I look for in qualifications and my answer is always same:

- no criminal history
- no evictions
- must make three times the rent
- credit score of at least six hundred

In some cities it's illegal to reject applicants due to past evictions or criminal history. I generally don't need to worry about that because I don't buy real estate in those cities.

Once a tenant is approved, they can move in the next weekend. I use a lease agreement that they can sign online. On move-in, they bring the rent money and security deposit.

I organize everything through email folders. I have one folder per property, one subfolder per unit, and another subfolder per tenant. In smaller properties I just have one subfolder per tenant. I use email folders because I can access them anywhere in the world. I've often needed to do this when problems arise while we're on vacation.

A copy of every message regarding the unit and tenant goes in that folder. If I have a text message exchange with the tenant, I screenshot those messages, email the screenshots to myself, and place them there. I also keep the background check and rental application in that folder. If anything happens, all this information is readily available anywhere. That's also of vital importance to have in case of a lawsuit but, knock on wood (please do so now for both of us), that's yet to happen.

Each month, I review leases for every unit. If the lease is yearly and due to expire within the period mandated by the city or state for rent increase notices, then I send a notice of rent increase. To determine how much to increase, I calculate the current market rent and then deduct ten percent. I intentionally stay below market so tenants are less likely to leave. For tenants who are month-to-month, I also increase their rents yearly and have the last date that I increased them in my notes, so I know when to reevaluate. How those rent increases are conveyed is dictated by city and state laws.

I have a landscaper work on a regular schedule to take care of the grounds. He sends a photo of the yard along with the bill when he's finished, and I send the check.

Since I can't drive to every building all the time, each has its own snitch who serves as my eyes and ears. Sometimes I listen to a bit more drama than I'd prefer, but I know everything that's going on. If unit 3B has a girlfriend living there without a lease, I'll know. If tenant 1A buys a Doberman, my snitch will tell me. I'll hear about every dispute and who hates whom. In retrospect, I probably would have done well at the KGB.

While you can't let tenants know how you know, you can find things out in public ways. If someone adds another tenant or adopts a dog or cat, schedule an inspection. Those details will be difficult to hide. Any additional occupants must go through screening to ensure they qualify based on your criteria. Recall my story with the "nurse" who was just living a few weeks with the tenant to assist with his back surgery. She was a drug dealer with an outstanding warrant.

I allow pets, but only up to a certain size and only with a pet deposit. In our state I must allow service animals with no questions asked and no pet deposit, but the rest must go through the process. The pet deposit will pay for extra cleaning when they move out, and the size restriction is for the safety of the neighbors and for cleanliness.

Either every quarter or twice a year I inspect the property. I examine the exterior, the interior common areas, and within the units. In my experience, tenants often don't report problems, especially when it's a leaking toilet and you're paying for the water. The regular inspections keep the property in good working order and prevent small problems from becoming big ones.

When contractors arrive for repairs, I'm never there. Instead, I have a contractor box waiting for them with the keys inside. I don't even have them send me pictures of the work, since if the job isn't done well the tenants will tell me. The only part of the transaction I manage is scheduling, which I'll arrange with the tenants. Because I use a contractor box to provide access, the tenants don't need to be home for the work, though many prefer to be.

Every year I reevaluate the rents. Do not let them level off for years on end or, at some point when you want to sell, you'll need to raise rents significantly to justify a higher sale price. Lower rents will devalue your building. I look up the going rate in the area, then keep my rents slightly below that price. I do this because I want to keep good tenants, and they won't go anywhere if nearby buildings aren't any cheaper.

The above are all elements of my system. Every notice or application I have saved: notice of rent increase, pay or vacate, stop smoking, stop throwing paint in the dumpster, do not throw raves, etc. I simply fill in the blanks and print them. If I'm unable to reach the property myself, I'll sometimes mail them to my snitch in the building.

Automation is the only way to keep your sanity. Once you have your system and you begin to scale to buildings not possible to manage yourself, you can then ensure your property manager follows a similar one. With your own system, you'll be in a better position to evaluate how good the manager is. It also enables you to verify that they'll keep your buildings in the same order you would yourself.

Making It Easier for Tenants to Pay

I'll digress for a moment to cover tenant payments. Most renters will be fine mailing a check to an address, placing the money in an envelope into a secure box (though not recommended due to the obvious theft risk), or paying it in person at an office. For some who work long day hours and don't have bank accounts, paying during regular office hours can be problematic.

It was a revelation to me upon becoming a landlord that so many people don't have bank accounts. Many also don't have a personal cell phone number. They purchase prepaid cards every month, so their numbers change. When they're late paying rent, getting ahold of them can be a challenge. What I've found works well for these situations is to offer payments via several in-store money transferers. Several pharmacies and some retailers, like Walmart, offer money wiring services. This is far more convenient than paying in person, as these businesses tend to be open later and on weekends. The following is how it works.

- You (landlord) pay a few hundred dollars to setup the account.
- You then provide the tenant a QR code
- The tenant walks into Walmart or a participating pharmacy and goes to the cashier
- The cashier scans the barcode and the tenant pays the rent, often in cash
- The money then goes directly to your bank account with the corresponding tenant information

What to Do with Vacant Units that Won't Rent

At times you'll have one or more units that just don't seem to rent. When that happens, start by taking new photos. You should always try to always take as professional photos as possible, but in this case try new angles and saturate the colors. Make sure the lights are on and the unit is as bright as possible. The following tips may help for photos.

- Make sure your verticals are correct, or in other words the doors, windows, and walls are parallel to the edges of the photo and go straight up, unless you're photographing staterooms on the Titanic.
- Try to place three walls in the photo, so tenants can see how large the room is.
- Don't cut off doors and windows in the frame.
- Close toilet seats and shower doors.

- Make sure all rooms are photographed and include all kitchen appliances and the washer or dryer, if a unit has them (or show the hookups).

Once you have new photos, create new ads. These should be fresh and you shouldn't just renew your existing listings. Place them on multiple sites like Craigslist, Zillow, Facebook Marketplace, and apartments.com.

The biggest thing you can do to rent units is to drop the price. Each month a unit sits vacant, you lose more money than you would have had you dropped its rent by $100. For example, if your unit is $1,000 per month and sits vacant for three months, then you've lost $3,000. In that year, you made $9,000 instead of $12,0000. Now, imagine you dropped it to $900 and rented it immediately. You'd then earn $11,700 per year. That's $2,700 extra you made just by dropping the price! Don't be greedy, as it will cost you more in the long run.

Working with Tenants

Your tenants are not slaves, and they aren't always going to do what you want. Differences will occur. How you deal with them will play a big part in the success of your building. Not every dispute will have a satisfying result. There are people who game the system.

During Covid, I had almost an entire building that stopped paying. It was a value-add, and I knew that every tenant would have to be evicted. However, before I could begin that work, the pandemic hit. Roughly 70 percent of the tenants stopped paying (the percentage would have been higher, but many units were already vacant), but I still had to pay the mortgage, taxes, insurance, and utilities. I ran at a loss on the building until the state resumed evictions.

Many of my clients also had similar tenants, but in states and cities that maintained eviction bans for longer. One of my clients had a triplex with a non-paying tenant. Even though this tenant was gainfully employed, she knew free rent when she saw it. To make matters worse, she then started heaping trash across the premises. The other tenants complained, but there was nothing my client could do. Eventually, due to an exceptionally long pause on evictions, my client chose to sell the building rather than face certain bankruptcy.

The situations above didn't have great resolutions, but most will be within your control. The keys are to have empathy while keeping a firm line, and never to yell. For example, if a tenant doesn't pay the rent, I'll post a pay-or-vacate notice. *Before* I move to eviction, however, I'll chat with the tenant about their reasons for nonpayment. While I can't let the tenant off for that month because all occupants of the building must be treated equally, I will suggest solutions.

There are many charity organizations that help down-on-their-luck individuals with rent. Get to know those available in your region. These include church groups and private charities. Have a list of these organizations ready and mail or email it to tenants who need it. Many times, they need help for just a short time.

Sometimes, if the issue is something serious like when a tenant is in the hospital, I admit I'll allow them to later catch up with the rent. Of course, I'll only do this once. If every time the tenant is late they claim it's because they were in the hospital, then I won't be so kind.

In terms of late payment penalties, while I now rigorously enforce them, I didn't always. When I self-managed, I was lenient in this area and allowed tenants to pay late without penalty if they paid. Some tenants consistently paid late due to their paycheck schedule. A few sent their rent like clockwork five days late every month. However, that doesn't scale, and now my property manager does enforce late fees.

More complicated disputes have arisen between some of my clients and tenants who simply didn't like each other. I think there's an expectation from some beginning investors that their tenants are just like them, and that's not the case. Usually, the income levels are disparate, and values may vary widely on various issues. If you are highly political, then you'll have to accept that some of your tenants will do things that may be against your moral or religious ideals in *your* building. Get over it. Your purpose is to provide shelter and the renter's purpose is to provide you income by paying for it. That's the extent of your relationship. Beyond that, they can do anything that's legal. And if they do something illegal, it's the police's job to enforce the laws, not yours.

Some of the most vicious disputes I've had to mediate between my clients and their tenants have been the pettiest ones. Maybe one renter parks in another's spot or keeps the outside messy, or smokes too close to the building. When this stuff happens, you really need to take a chill pill.

If you'd like a tenant to do something, ask nicely. When you do so, provide the reasons why you're asking. Perhaps their trash is bringing rats. Maybe an oil leak from their truck is a safety or environmental hazard. On the flip side, if you find yourself struggling to come up with a reason, question whether it's even worth making the request. Don't get involved in your tenants' lives if you can avoid it.

When the dispute is between the tenants, you should generally try not to get involved. Perhaps one tenant is playing his stereo too loudly. Are there noise ordinances in the city? If so, then the tenant should bring the problem up with the police and the city, not with you. You should avoid at all costs playing peacemaker. You're not their mommy and they can't run to you crying. You're their landlord. They need to either resolve matters like this themselves or, if the matter is serious enough, with the authorities.

Resolving Tenant Disputes

At some point, you'll have a tenant who successfully manages to piss off several others. When your good tenants start leaving the building due to this conflict, you have a problem. Your options are often limited.

While your lease should spell out exact behavior that will violate the terms, it can be difficult to evict for those reasons. Some cities even restrict the causes for eviction, so any avenue there might be closed. You should, of course, ask the tenant to stop the malicious behavior, but what if he simply refuses?

If the tenant is month-to-month, the simplest approach is to terminate the lease. Before doing so, verify with your lawyer that this action is possible in your area, as some cities require a minimum notice or outlaw the practice completely. In the case of a yearly lease, provide the required notice that it will not be renewed.

I've had bad apples in my own properties and it's just not worth the effort to keep them. In the long run they'll cost you a fortune due to the constant vacancies caused by their behavior. Consult your attorney on the legal and most cost-effective way to remove them.

Be Direct, But Listen

My husband Joe is more than happy to admit that he encourages me to invest out of state because he doesn't want me managing buildings myself. Perhaps it's the immigrant in me, but I have no fear of asking *any* tenant to pay. I've knocked on doors where huge men answered, and I've seen their eyes bulge when I ask plainly, "Where's my rent?"

I still do that when I fly in. When it comes to rent, there's no beating around the bush: If they haven't paid, then why? You promised in writing to pay me that rent, so where is it? Every landlord will need to do this at one time or another.

When I managed my own buildings, some tenants would call me a "mad Russian" (or, I'm sure, worse names) behind my back. I really don't care. The only thing I do care about is that tenants pay their rent on time and take care of my unit.

Chapter 13

I believe that while my tenants fear me to a degree, they also trust me because I'm firm yet fair. One time, I had just finished showing a unit to a young woman. I hadn't run her application yet because she hadn't submitted one. As she drove off, one of my current tenants whispered that he wanted to talk.

I'm sure you're familiar with Dwayne "The Rock" Johnson, who has been in many of my favorite movies. He's a big guy. My tenant looked like his bigger, meaner brother. He appeared scary but was the nicest guy and a great tenant. After he saw she'd left, he approached me.

The poor guy was nearly in tears. It turned out that he knew this woman. They'd previously had a relationship and she had *abused* him physically and verbally. She'd been stalking him since he'd left her, and he was terribly afraid of her still and would be forced to move if she rented the unit next to his. I thanked him for the information, then informed her I'd rented the unit to someone else.

On another occasion, a tenant called me in tears. Her boyfriend, who was also on the lease and lived with her, had been beating her and she'd reached a breaking point. Although this wasn't in the landlord job description, I guided her through filing for a restraining order. When he left but she was unable to pay the rent, I let her break the lease without repercussions.

Managing your own properties can be exhausting, both physically and mentally. Although you should never meddle in your tenants' lives, you'll inevitably learn far more than you would wish. At some point, you'll just have too many units to handle on your own. At that point, you'll need to hire a property manager, which is the subject of the next chapter.

Chapter 14
Property Managers

SOME MAY ARGUE that honest property managers are a myth. "They're an impossibility," I've been told. In truth, I was starting to believe this myself but then I found the perfect manager.

She was new to the game then, with fifty or so doors under her belt, but I knew right away she had the skills to make it. Fast forward to today, she's grown to having a large and productive staff, and we're still going strong. We've been through a lot together, both in business and on a personal level.

Why It's Difficult to Find a Good Manager

No matter how long someone argues, there *are* great property managers out there. You just have to find the right one.

The overriding problem is that many property managers use an economic model that doesn't favor your business. Many charge you not only a percentage of the rents, but also add fees for moving new tenants in and evicting problem tenants. Under this model, they're not motivated to find long-term renters for the highest priced units. Instead, they'll fill units quickly with the first person that has a pulse. It doesn't matter if the new tenants don't pay because they'll earn one bonus when they evict, and another when they refill the vacancy.

It's no secret that good property managers are difficult to find. In contrast to managers who seem to revel in vacancies are those who wind up working more for the tenants than for you. This is a major issue when purchasing properties, as more than once I've seen the sellers' property manager sign a tenant on a two-year lease at far below market value days before closing. As a rule, your contract language should state that you must approve all leases. I also advise that you ask the sellers to keep vacant units unless the total vacancy for the building is under 90 percent, which could threaten agency financing. We know that if the sellers fill those vacancies, they aren't motivated to find someone decent at the market rate.

Finding a Good Property Manager

Now that I've properly scared you about property managers, how do you go about finding the rare breed of good ones? Well, as I detailed in the previous chapter, it starts by you learning the ropes yourself.

There is no other way you can understand the intricacies of this business. While experience will enable you to find great property managers, it will also provide great context on what they can and cannot do. You *will* have vacancies and evictions. It's simply not possible to predict when and how many with certainty. While you can obviously take steps to minimize them, you'll never eliminate evictions completely. After you've managed buildings yourself, you'll know firsthand what lies in the realm of possible.

Merging Systems

When you first meet with a property manager, you should learn what system he uses. Assuming you have perfected your craft, how does his system differ from your own? Is he able and willing to change things to match your system?

One policy I had to change when I hired a property manager was related to late charges. When I managed myself, I tended to be relaxed in this area. Only those who were habitually late, and then very late, received a late charge. Otherwise, I was understanding that things can be tough, and if the tenant told me in advance that the payment would be late and provided an estimate when it would arrive, I let them off. I did this because I preferred steady tenants who eventually paid to constantly shuffling units.

When I switched to hiring a property manager, this leniency had to stop. She managed far too many units to keep track of this. She'll still factor client communication into how quickly things move to eviction, but if you're late by the number of days stipulated in the lease, then she adds a late fee.

One aspect where she did change her system to meet mine, though, was in working with charitable organizations. This has been a great help in avoiding evictions. If a tenant doubts he'll be able to pay the next rent due to unemployment or extreme circumstances, she'll provide a sheet with local organizations that can help. During Covid, she also provided instructions on how to apply for government assistance. She assists with filling out paperwork and gathering all supporting documentation, then helps them submit it.

Again, had I not managed properties myself and learned this, I wouldn't have known about these organizations or how to work with them.

Section 8

Since I'm on the subject of charities, it's time now to discuss the most widespread one—Section 8. To some people, the very name brings up absolute horror. For those not in the know, it's a federal housing assistance program.

Chapter 14

Do I recommend allowing Section 8? That depends.

First, local laws may *require* you to accept Section 8, so you may have no choice. The primary advantage of this program, and the reason I accept it in all my buildings, is that you're guaranteed rent.

The way Section 8 works is roughly as follows: First, renters must apply for this program. There are strict salary requirements, and it can take years to be approved. Those who are on Section 8 are very motivated to keep it because violations may prevent them from ever receiving it again.

They come to you as a normal prospective tenant, though early in the process there must be an agreement that you accept Section 8. Either you place this information in the listing, tell them when asked, or it is assumed based on local regulations. You are allowed and encouraged to background check and screen these tenants just as you would anyone else.

One disadvantage with Section 8 is that you may not receive the amount you request for the unit. The government has price ranges based on location, size, and other parameters. These are not a secret and may be found either online or by requesting a potential tenant's voucher. If your rent falls within the range allowed by Section 8, you're fine. Otherwise, the rent is lowered to that range. In my experience, their ranges are usually fair market value. I once had to provide proof that my unit was worth what I was asking for it. The case manager wanted to see comparable units in the area that supported my asking price. When I provided that information, they adjusted the tenant's voucher to fair market value. So far, I've never had them reject my listed rent on a unit.

The rent is then divided between the tenant's portion and the government's. Sometimes Section 8 pays the entire rent. You will *always* receive the government portion on the first of each month, though in rare situations they can be delayed, such as a shutdown due to political impasse. The tenant must pay his portion as any other tenant does. If he doesn't pay, you're allowed to evict, though in practice you should alert their Section 8 case manager first. Tenants are motivated to pay because an eviction will often end their participation in the program.

To ensure your building is a good environment for the tenant, Section 8 will perform an inspection. You are required to make any repairs they request in order to participate. They mainly look for health hazards and safety issues. This is one of the biggest complaints landlords have with the program because they'll often call out the smallest things, such as a leak under the sink or cracked grout in the shower.

These inspections will occur annually and any issues found must be promptly fixed or the rent is withheld. There's a positive and a negative to this. On the good side, it's more likely that major issues will be discovered earlier. On the bad side, most of the issues found are trivial and the effort to get a contractor to the unit to perform such a tiny job is greater than the actual repair or cost.

Perhaps the biggest gripe landlords have with Section 8 is the perception that the tenants on the program will cause problems. This isn't my experience. First, you're allowed to screen them just like any other tenant. Second, these people are on thin ice in terms of causing problems. Too many issues and they're off the program.

Interviewing Property Managers

Going back to property managers, you've now contacted someone who's interested in managing your buildings. What do you ask in the interview?

Easily the most important question is how they structure their fees. Most charge a percentage of gross rents, but don't assume that one manager is cheaper than another due to a lower percentage. The following are other possible fees.

Eviction charges – Yes, if the property manager chooses the wrong tenant, you not only pay the legal fees but you'll pay the manager a fee to handle the process.

Unit rental charges – Each time there's a vacancy, you'll pay the property manager to fill it.

Contractor surcharge – Some managers act as a general contractor for repairs and charge you a percentage on top of the contractor costs, usually 10 or 15 percent.

Software charges – Most managers use a software package to provide reports and track units. If so, they charge you the licensing fees.

Personally, I don't like services that nickel-and-dime me, so I don't use them. I pay a flat fee for everything. It's a bit higher than other managers' flat fees but I feel it comes out to less in the long run.

Besides understanding the fees, you need to quantify what duties your property managers are performing. Some property managers only collect rents, transfer the money to your account, and provide a report. These are the cheapest ones. They do nothing in terms of showing units, following up with tenants on late rent, or handling repairs and maintenance.

For these tasks, they usually request that you hire a full-time person in the complex. The problem is that staff's salary can be quite high, and the work from a few dozen units doesn't justify a dedicated person. I would also argue that interfacing with tenants is the most taxing part of the job, so why should I pay an eight percent fee to a manager who only collects and deposits checks?

In addition to asking how their fees are structured, it's also useful to ask these questions:

What is your success rate for keeping tenants?

Do you have a network of contractors you use?

Are any of them full-time?

Which software do you use?

Do you have other people, such as attorneys, pest control companies, and landscapers you can refer?

Ideally, mention a specific property you would like to buy. Ask the property manager if she knows that building. While this skill differs by geography, I've found that in metro areas of roughly 300,000 people, experienced property managers are familiar with most properties. Even if they don't manage a property themselves, they somehow learn that "This one has plumbing problems" and "That one's owned by so-and-so."

Ask the prospective manager how much rent you should receive for a given unit. A good manager will give a figure in the right ballpark. If their number is very low, you should be concerned. Many managers intentionally rent units at low prices in order to fill them easily. These are typically the same ones who charge fees for renting vacant units. Those who charge a flat percentage across collections are motivated to seek higher rents and tenants who can afford to pay them.

Our property manager continually surprises us. One day she called me to say she'd rented a unit. I thanked her, then asked how much she got for it. I nearly fell off my chair. "How much!?" It was mind boggling how much rents had climbed. We'd barely owned the property for a year and were already achieving rents that were 20 percent higher than our pro forma! We never had to push her to reach those rents. I nicknamed her "the price pusher." and she giggles and laughs, then tries to surprise us by the time our next monthly call arrives.

Working with Your Property Manager

One aspect that can't be quantified is how smoothly you and your property manager collaborate. You'll need to get along with your property manager, and that's easily more important than how you get along with anyone else on your team. I've squabbled plenty of times with my agent and lender, but my manager and I always need to be on the same page. There's a reason for this: at times things can get *very* stressful.

I recall one day during our monthly meeting when she mentioned that a car had run through our metal fence and damaged a brick wall. The driver had been drunk and was arrested. He didn't have insurance. I swear, we maybe talked about this for a minute. She already had a contractor quoting the work. It sucked, but there was no way to get our money back. The deductible on our insurance was too high. A lawyer was useless. This guy didn't have anything. The only proper way to handle the situation was to fix the problem and move on with our lives.

Another week, three of our tenants died. They were all separate causes, in different buildings, and didn't know each other. Again, there wasn't much involvement necessary on our part. The police asked for our security camera footage in one case, and we handed it over. Authorities had removed the bodies (more about that in Chapter 16), we cleaned up, contacted relatives to handle personal items, then turned the units.

These aren't horror stories. They're part of being a landlord, but you're in trouble if you have a property manager who freaks out when these things happen. You both need to be easygoing and efficient when dealing with issues, even when the issues aren't easy.

Eventually, your property manager should turn into a good friend. Though you may not show up for each other's parties, you'll have been through wars with each other. Up next are several far less friendly entities you'll unfortunately have to deal with. It's time to discuss utilities.

Chapter 15
Utilities

THIS IS A utility chapter. You transferred the utilities to your name when you took possession of the property, right? Seriously? That's one of the worst mistakes you can make! Imagine your tenants just sitting around and being peaceful when… wham! Their lights go off or their water stops running. They can't cook. They can't shower. It's either hot and they're roasting alive inside, or it's cold and they're freezing to death, and it's all because you forgot to transfer the utilities and the previous owner closed the account when he received the bill.

Their hands are reaching for it now… reaching for the phone. They're going to call their friends and complain, and that you can live with. Sure, they'll call your property manager, but switching the account and turning the utilities back on can take days. Eventually, one friend is going to suggest they call someone else, and after so many days of shivering in a room with no lights and heat, they're going to take that friend's advice. They're going to call a lawyer.

The lawyer they call is not going to be the nice type you meet occasionally at dinner parties who constantly apologizes for being a lawyer. No. That lawyer's going to lick his chops when your tenant calls, and he's going to look you up. He's going to see what you own and calculate your net worth. When he's done, he's going to smile and say, "I think we can get a bit more."

Transferring Utilities

Don't let that lawyer get to you. Transfer the utilities the instant you take possession. Even before closing, make sure you have a list of all the relevant utilities, their phone numbers, and understand the process for transferring. You can often arrange this in advance with the utility provider. Just tell them the date services should commence, provide them with all financial information, and they'll carry out the transfer on the day of closing, though I recommend calling them on that day just to make sure. I cannot stress more how important this is.

There's a common misconception that escrow handles all the utilities. They do not. In some cities, escrow will clear out all utilities, while in others they only clear out those capable of placing liens. This means that the utilities *may* be paid off. It doesn't mean they're in your name. and the instant the previous owner receives a bill, he's going to be pissed and will have no issues closing the account and letting the utility shut off power or water on you.

Normally, I embellish my advice with true stories from the field, but in this case I cannot. Why? Have you ever heard of post-traumatic stress? Yes. The last thing I want is people I admire curling up into a ball on their bed when they're reading this and crying, "Please don't let it happen again. Please don't. Please don't."

Don't let this be you. Get on top of things and make sure utilities are transferred. In some cities, utility companies will require a bond before they provide your building with service. This bond protects the utility provider from you not paying and may be the equivalent of a year in payments. It can be in the thousands of dollars. While utility companies will gladly tell you the amount necessary, it's your job to pay this in time for utilities to transfer, and in some cities they have no qualms about turning vital services off for a late payment by even a single hour. When you sell the property, the utility provider will return your bond to you minus any unpaid balance. In some respects, you're giving them an interest-free loan.

Where the utilities are paid by the tenant, you have less of a concern. There, you typically pay only garbage for the whole building, and electric, sewer, and water for any common areas. When a tenant moves out, he's responsible for closing his account unless he wants to pay for the next tenant, which is very generous. When a new tenant moves in, provide her with the relevant utility information, but otherwise setting up the account is her responsibility.

In some communities the utility won't shut off service if the tenant stops paying but will instead bill the landlord. Since utility companies can and will place a lien against your building, you will need to pay that bill. Make sure to understand whether your service providers can do this, and stipulate what you'll do in the lease. I will bill tenants when this happens. If a tenant has neglected to pay their utility bills when moving out—which happens often - I'll deduct the amount from their security deposit.

In general, I've found utility companies to be bureaucratic but otherwise fair to deal with. There is one third party vendor, though, that has been a source of frustration for years. They're the mafia of the real estate industry and represent the only time I've completely lost my temper. I'm speaking, of course, about laundry machine companies.

Laundry Servicers

Laundry servicers come with the property. If you really wanted to, you could build your own solar power station and stop using the city's electric. You could buy a reservoir and divert it for your water. You could even bulldoze your entire building and construct something completely different. You can do anything you want, except use a different laundry company.

Their contracts can be nearly impossible to escape. It doesn't matter that you never signed a contract with them. They're inherited with the building and the contracts last an extraordinarily long time, then automatically roll over into another impossibly long contract.

I've seen drastically different earnings from various laundry servicers. In one city, I have two buildings on the same street, each with a different provider. One building is half the size of the other but generates double the laundry profits.

With many laundry providers, you have very little say over the makeup of your machines. *They* decide how many are necessary no matter what you suggest. In the non-performing case above, I know the reason is that there aren't enough machines so tenants wash their laundry elsewhere. Every few months, I call to ask for more machines and the laundry servicers promise to send someone. Two years later, I still haven't received the machines. I probably never will. That servicer will provide one washer and one dryer for roughly fifty units until the earth ends, and then thousands of years later aliens will visit our planet and one will happen across the ruins of my building and there will be the laundry provider, and that poor alien will inherit the contract.

There is hope for you. Not all laundry providers are sadistic. Some aren't that bad, and with those you can even ask for new machines. They'll usually ask you to sign a new contract before they provide them, but then you can negotiate how much of the proceeds you receive. Make sure you thoroughly read through the terms and conditions because they'll likely change from what you had before.

Newer laundry machines no longer use coins. They take either credit cards or an app, which is preferable since scammers may attempt to install a hidden camera or skimmer on your machines to read the numbers from people's cards. Newer machines have no coins to steal, which is the leading cause of laundry machine damage. They also look a lot cooler, in my opinion.

Given the issues with laundry machine providers, is it worth contracting with them? Well, remember that you may have no choice. However, if you have a choice, and you do your homework by obtaining opinions from other landlords before hiring any firm, they're far preferable to managing the machines yourself. Tenants can be brutal to laundry machines, and you'll spend a lot of time maintaining them. You may also be stuck with older coin-based machines that are constantly vandalized.

Make sure to secure your laundry room. Unless your property is in an extremely good area (and then I'd question why your units don't have machines themselves), laundry rooms are prime targets for the homeless. In some cities, it can be non-trivial to evict someone who decides to make your laundry facility their home. In any case, it's still a major pain to call the police and clean up the room.

In my buildings, I install a lock on the laundry room and then provide all tenants with the key. Make sure that your laundry room door swings shuts and locks by itself, or tenants will leave the door unlocked and a homeless person will invite themselves in. In an added complication, if homeless people move into your laundry room, servicers will usually refuse to come. This can halt laundry service to the entire building, so it's best to stay ahead of the situation.

If you have someone who cleans up the grounds, make sure he checks the laundry room door each day, morning and night. I've had problems in my buildings where a sympathetic tenant will intentionally leave the door open for the homeless, and tenants sometimes prop doors open when friends are expected. If your grounds person makes sure to shut the door, or even better notifies you who is leaving it open, it's more likely to remain shut.

Should You Bundle Utilities?

How should you have tenants pay for utilities? As I mentioned earlier, if the units are individually metered, the answer is easy. The tenants set up their own accounts and are on the hook for the utilities they use.

What if the units aren't individually metered? In that case, you can do one of two things:

1. Divide the utility bills by the number of units and add that to each unit's rent. Note that bills will change every month
2. Increase the rent by some set amount and include utilities

The first option is fraught with problems. You'll need to calculate the utility total each month, then relay to every unit what their share is. That means tenants can't pay you until you provide this number, and they can't set up automatic payments. In my experience, this leads to more late payments and evictions. It isn't worth it.

I far prefer the second option. In the second option, you increase rents by enough of a buffer to cover the anticipated bills. If you do this, try to steer clear of leases longer than a year because you can't increase rents every time utilities raise their rates. Still, bundling everything together is the far simpler option.

Unfortunately, with both options you'll often have someone who uses a ton of one resource, usually water. This will raise your bills and potentially everyone else's, but there's little you can do other than replace shower heads and toilets with more efficient models. Depending on your local regulations, you *may* not be able to renew a lease if a unit's consumption is excessive.

Finally, should you just change the building to be separately metered? This is a question for your contractor. If you're doing a complete gutting, where every unit is already down to the studs and all electrical and plumbing are accessible, it may be doable. Usually the costs are prohibitive, especially if most units are already rented out. However, every building is different, so consult with a reputable contractor if you want to know. We've done this in smaller buildings of two or three units.

Now that we've handled utilities, it's time to address the grimmer sides of the business.

Chapter 16
Death and Taxes

THIS WON'T BE your favorite chapter. No one likes either death or taxes, so I bundled them to get it done and over with. We'll start with taxes, since that's where the most questions arise.

Contrary to what you might think, the government *wants* you to invest in real estate. For that reason, tax laws *favor* those who do so. In fact, you can save hundreds of thousands or even millions of dollars by investing in real estate. This is not a tax book, nor am I a CPA. Therefore, the advice given here will be at a very high level. I recommend you read specialized books on real estate tax concerns and hire a CPA who specializes in real estate.

I cannot overemphasize the importance of hiring an appropriate CPA. Early on, we didn't have a CPA who really knew real estate and our resulting decisions were poor, to say the least. Real estate involves special concerns. While a regular CPA can be great for filling out your taxes if you sell gizmos online or work a day job at a chicken farm, he's not in a position to give you decent advice for real estate.

The following are words to mention to your real estate CPA: cost segregation, 1031 exchange, and dealer. These are not just buzzwords but are constructs you *will* use. Imagine you need brain surgery and your doctor starts looking at your stomach. You ask him why and he answers "Aah. I forgot. They're in different places for everyone." Would you want him to operate on you? If a CPA doesn't know these terms and how they apply to you, run away. Maybe excuse yourself and thank him for his time, but don't use him for your investment taxes or you'll be very sorry.

Moving back to taxes, the tax rules were written specifically to stimulate the economy by encouraging good economic behavior. Investing in real estate is good economic behavior. You're improving buildings and hence your tenants' quality of life. You're hiring property managers, contractors, lawyers, landscapers, and a whole host of others. This is an activity the government wants to promote.

1031 Exchanges

The most famous way the government promotes this is through the construct called a 1031 Exchange. The idea here is you have one property, and you sell it to buy another. Recall Chapter 5 and eROI. At some point, the ratio will be so high that even your cat will be handing you listings. I once sold a house that was earning $6,000 a year and bought a thirty-unit multifamily that earns $120,000. That move made sense, and I used a 1031 Exchange to make it happen.

To use a 1031 Exchange you'll need to plan, as you do for most tax advantages. I've had clients come to me after they've sold their building and ask me to help with a 1031 Exchange, and I could only sadly shake my head. You need to set this up *before* you sell the building. The steps work as follows.

1. You decide to sell the building. You're going to need to find two people:

    a. A real estate agent who *knows* 1031 Exchanges. Please, please, ask her how many exchanges she's done both for herself and for her clients. Too many times I've seen agents who didn't know what they were doing royally screw over their clients. Note that if a real estate agent tells you that she has facilitators who handle all the details, thank her and hang up. A facilitator alone is *not sufficient* for handling a 1031 Exchange. You need an agent who is intimately familiar with handling the deadlines so that the facilitator *and* agent can dance together and stay ahead of them.

    b. An "exchange facilitator." This is a company that specializes in the legal aspects of a 1031 Exchange. If you don't know of one, your agent can provide you with a referral.

2. List your building and get it under contract. Your exchange facilitator will need to work with your escrow to ensure the proceeds go to a special holding account.

3. Once your building closes, you have forty-five days to identify one or more properties for the exchange. This can be a very stressful time. If you fail to identify a property, your funds will be held up for 180 days and you'll pay taxes. That will suck. If your agent isn't out there helping you find a new property *before* your own is under contract, then fire her because this isn't going to work.

4. Once you've identified one or more properties, you have 180 days to close on them.

Assuming all the stars have aligned and the process above works, you can roll the equity you have in your first building into your second. Technically, you're only *deferring* the taxes you must pay, since if you sell the second building you'll have to pay on the equity for all buildings down the line. However, many people keep 1031 exchanging into larger buildings until they die, at which time two things happen. First, you'll no longer care. Second, anyone who receives the buildings in your estate takes ownership with a basis equal to the current list price, so they pay no taxes. (I believe buildings may need to be in a trust to be tax exempt. Consult with your tax attorney).

The efficacy of a 1031 Exchange depends highly on the corporate structure where you place it. The answer usually is an LLC, but verify this with your CPA before you proceed. Note that your CPA will need to be familiar with 1031 Exchanges in order to properly file your taxes. It was during our first 1031 Exchange that our CPA fired us because we had become too complicated. When we later hired one who knew what he was doing, we learned how many costly mistakes we had made.

I highly recommend you take advantage of 1031 Exchanges when trading up buildings. The primary disadvantage is the forty-five-day identification period, but it's not difficult to handle that. First, *before* you even start the process, look at the market and make sure there are several buildings you would like to move on. I say several, because you need to have confidence that you can find something in those forty-five days.

Note also that you can "extend" that forty-five day deadline by getting something under contract before your own property closes. While most sellers frown on contingent offers, if you already are under contract and have passed due diligence, there will be much more confidence in your ability to perform. Sometimes an agent can even extend the closing of your first property by a few weeks in order to buy you more time.

Another option is to make an offer on the target building first with a late closing date, then list yours. This can be tricky to complete within the time limits, but if you offer your property for a fair price in a good market, it should be possible.

Note that a 1031 Exchange may complicate refinancing. While it *is* possible for the BRRRR method and 1031 Exchanges to exist together, you must be careful that all the funds pulled from the refinance can be used to purchase properties. Consult a CPA familiar with exchanges *before* you refinance in order to verify that any funds pulled out are not taxable, or you'll ruin the tax savings of your original exchange.

Opportunity Zones

Another tax-advantaged program is what are currently called "Opportunity Zones." These are areas specified by the government that offer tax incentives in terms of reduction and deferral of capital gains. In exchange for this reduction in taxes, you're required to invest at least a certain amount into the property. You can ask your CPA what these numbers are.

Personally, I've never been enticed much with opportunity zones. The amount you must invest into the property can be considerable, and I tend to be cheap. I'm also not keen to lock up even more cash in a property via repairs, and strongly prefer to use rental profits to fix up a building over time. Therefore, even though opportunity zones are focused on similar value-add properties as those that are my bread and butter, I've avoided them. However, they may suit your needs.

Self-Directed Investment Accounts

Though it's a more advanced topic, it's possible to utilize your retirement accounts for purchasing real estate. The rules for accomplishing this are complex, but the following are a few high-level details.

- You must hire a company to handle the account for you. This is akin to hiring a facilitator for a 1031 Exchange.
- Certain people will be labeled as "disqualified." This is usually yourself and your relatives. Disqualified individuals may have nothing to do with the properties contained in the self-directed account. They can provide no services, even for

free. For example, you can't have your kids mow the lawn at the property, which I'm sure will upset them.
- All earnings from the account must return to the self-directed account.
- You cannot add your own funds to the self-directed account. For example, you can't help the account with the down payment for a property. It is possible for a self-directed account to receive a loan on a property, but there are strict guidelines and a limited number of banks who will work with self-directed accounts. Consult your facilitator for the details.

It is technically possible to roll over other types of retirement accounts, such as a 401k, into a self-directed retirement account. Search for "Solo 401k" for more information. Keep in mind that the above guidelines are only a sampling. Although it's certainly doable, you'll need to hire a company that specializes in this and follow their directions to the letter in order to avoid the entire account being considered taxable by the IRS.

Cost Segregation

Cost segregation can provide even more savings than 1031 Exchanges. This is something that sounds shady when you first hear about it but is perfectly legal. The idea is based on depreciation: Each year you can deduct a certain percentage of your building's value. Note that this is the value of any structures on your property and does not include the land value. Over time, your building will degrade, so you can deduct the percentage of your building that degrades that year, which is called depreciation. This is typically done over twenty-seven and a half years.

With cost segregation, you're saying that certain parts of your building will degrade much faster than others. For example, appliances will not usually last thirty years. You'll need to replace them sooner than that. The tax laws, in fact, stipulate how many years you can depreciate certain things.

You must hire a company that specializes in cost segregation to create a report for the IRS that divides your building into those components that can be depreciated sooner rather than later. These people will literally count the number of doorknobs, kitchen cabinets, drawers, light fixtures, and trees on your property. You may think I'm joking, but this is exactly what they'll do. You'll learn more strange facts about your building than you ever conceived of through your cost segregation report.

The results can be staggering. Instead of deducting 3 percent of your building in your first year, you may be able to deduct 40 percent. This can lead to a huge tax break. Not only can you counter all your gains in rents, but if you're a real estate professional (defined later), you can counter large personal gains. You may be able to counter, for example, the gains from the sale of stocks.

Cost segregation is very much an "eat your cake and have it too" approach, since technically you're not depreciating anything less but are just front-loading it. However, the money you *don't* need to pay taxes this year can be used to buy more buildings, which in turn can be cost segregated.

The rules for cost segregation, and how much you can gain from it, vary from person to person. Consult your CPA (who specializes in real estate and knows cost segregation) and have him calculate the estimated gains before you pay for this service. Cost segregation companies will provide a rough estimate of your gains before performing the job, but it's up to your CPA to determine how much of that you can actually deduct. If you're a real estate professional, you can typically deduct more.

Chapter 16

Real Estate Professionals

When it comes to the IRS, who qualifies as a real estate professional? Many believe that obtaining a real estate license and hanging your license somewhere is the only thing necessary, but that isn't true. At the time of writing, two basic things must be true to achieve this tax status.

First, you must spend more than fifty percent of your total working hours on real estate. Therefore, if you're a lawyer full-time, you won't qualify for this status unless you're a lawyer who has no clients. If you *do* work full-time in real estate, or you're retired, this status is easier to prove.

Second, you must spend at least 750 hours per year in real estate activities, not including the time you spend searching for that next property. If you are not a full-time real estate agent at a brokerage, then you'll need to document the hours you spend. Technically, you always need to document your hours, but the IRS typically doesn't ask for proof from someone who is obviously doing this as her main employment.

Once you achieve this magical status, you're allowed to write off losses such as depreciation on your taxes. When you add in cost segregation, this can mean major gains. Perhaps you made a few hundred thousand when you sold some stocks. It's possible to balance this with cost segregation and pay no taxes. Read that last part again. Here, I'll help you: Pay no taxes.

If you've ever read those stories of slimy politicians who make gazillions of dollars but pay no taxes, this is how. There's nothing wrong with it because, as I said before, you're participating in monetary activities encouraged by our government. Yes, you're being an awesome patriot by trading in apartment buildings. You're participating in the American Way.

Dealer Designation

There are real estate activities, though, that the government *does not* like. They frown on flippers, for example. They do this through a concept called a "dealer." In this case, instead of drugs and cars, you're dealing houses. If you sell enough houses in a given year, the IRS will label you as a dealer. You don't want this.

Why? Because then everything you earn will be taxable per the usual brackets. You won't qualify for all those wonderful exemptions and a profitable sale will zoom you straight up to the highest bracket where you'll be murdalized in taxes. At that point, you become a piggy bank for the government.

Unfortunately, what defines a dealer is a bit arbitrary. The IRS provides no clear-cut line, but the more properties you sell in a year, the more likely they'll designate you as a dealer. Evidently, the IRS doesn't feel that houses should be peddled like sports cards. They should be relatively uncommon purchases and sales.

If your goal is to flip properties, check with your CPA before you get in too deep. In fact, I recommend checking with your CPA before you sell anything in order to analyze potential tax ramifications. The last thing you want is to find out when it's too late.

I'm going to say something now that may rub people the wrong way. Several times I've earned over a million dollars and paid absolutely nothing in taxes. I know some specific people who will say I didn't do my "civic duty," but I counter that numerous people depended on me for their living that year. I created jobs. I enabled people to feed their families and I provided shelter for hundreds of people. Because I did this, the government rewarded me with no taxes.

I cannot stress this more: the government *wants* you to invest. They *want* you to stimulate the economy, and if you do so they will *reward* you through lower taxes. Until you understand that philosophy, you won't truly be an investor.

Chapter 16

How to Handle Deaths in Your Units

I've just proved that the accepted fact of death and taxes being unavoidable isn't true. The latter is technically escapable, while the former is not. This is a subject few authors really like to write about because it's morbid. However, I like you. You bought my book and I appreciate that, so I'm not going to let you frantically search for what to do when one of your tenants passes away in your unit.

People are going to die in your buildings. That's a fact. Statistics say that the more units you own, the higher the odds that one renter will pass away in a given calendar year. The first order of business is to not get emotional. These things happen.

Once, my husband and I were on vacation when one of my tenants' daughters called, frantic that her mother wasn't answering the door. I tried to call the tenant, but received no answer, so I sent someone over. There was no sound. Finally, we called the police for a wellness check. I sent one of my colleagues from my real estate office with them.

"Is she dead?" I texted my colleague.

She nearly blew up at me. "How can you be so calm! OMG!" She was nearly in tears. The police pounded on the door, threatened to push it down, and the tenant finally showed up.

Of course, I haven't always gotten off that easy. I've had people drink themselves to death, overdose, die of old age, and worse. When that happens, you call 911 and they dispatch you to the correct authority, and they handle the deceased. If it appears to be a crime scene, the police will block off the area and your only responsibility will be to answer any questions they may have. They'll then remove the body to the morgue, but I don't really learn the details, nor is it the landlord's job to know.

Unless you had some paranormal lawyer draw up the lease, or there's another tenant still alive in the unit, that tenant's lease is now over. You'll need to contact the next of kin, who hopefully are listed on the deceased tenant's application, and arrange for them to remove any personal effects. The laws vary by state, so don't throw anything away until the family has been through the unit and you're confident you've followed the relevant laws.

Complications arise if there's still… something… left of the person. Please, oh please, *do not* send in a normal cleaner to handle it. There are professional biohazard teams that handle jobs like this. Call your insurance company, who will in turn hire a specialist in human remains removal. These companies are very expensive, though your insurance should help with some of the cost. Once this is handled, the rest of the cleanup can be accomplished by a typical cleaner.

One common mistake landlords make in these situations is believing that there's no next of kin. Take the story of one of my tenants, who I'll call Norman. When Norman filled out his application, he didn't list an emergency contact. I asked him about this, and he replied that there was no one. He had no immediate or extended family. I said he had to put someone down, so he put his manager from work.

Several years later, Norman drank so much that he collapsed on the street and was taken to the hospital. No one knew anything. For weeks, there was no Norman. Did he die? No one had any idea because hospitals only provide that information to family, and he had none. We called the manager, but Norman had retired and the manager didn't know anything. After some time, we decided to move all his possessions to storage, then remodel the unit.

Literally the next day, a man arrived at the building and asked where Norman's belongings were. We told him what we had heard, and he replied that Norman was doing better, was in the hospital recovering, and that he was Norman's cousin. Wait, what? I thought he had no one.

We finished remodeling the unit, put all of Norman's stuff back, and he was so very happy to come back to an upgraded and beautiful

Chapter 16

place. Of course, we never mentioned that we remodeled it because we thought he was dead and wanted to achieve a higher rent, but things could have ended a lot worse if we had gone through an eviction (he hadn't paid since he was hospitalized) or had permanently disposed of his things because he had no kin and no one to claim his items.

I strongly recommend you make every effort to obtain emergency contacts for new tenants. If someone does pass away, store any possessions not claimed by family for thirty to sixty days (or whatever your local law suggests) just in case.

Once the mess is removed, you can treat the unit like any other vacancy. Some localities have laws about disclosing any deaths in the unit to potential renters, but most don't. Note that the cause of death is private, so don't share it with tenants. I once had a tenant who surpassed Norman and *did* drink himself to death. The tenants next door thought he was murdered and broke their leases. I couldn't enlighten them, so I just let them break their leases. It was in my best interest anyway since I was in the process of raising rents significantly.

I hope this chapter has set you up for some of the more unsavory things in real estate. Taxes, in fact, are actually a bright spot. You can use real estate investing to pay less. In terms of tenant deaths, they happen. As a landlord, your job is simply to clean things up and move on.

Planning for property management, utilities, and taxes needs to be handled *before* you close on a property. Now that I've covered those topics, let's move on to closing the deal.

Chapter 17
Closing the Deal

CLOSING IS ALL about preparation and having a great team. There is a high probability that *someone* will have a great deal of stress at a given closing, but with the right team in place there are fair odds that it won't be you.

Timelines

The time necessary to close varies widely by property. I've seen as short as one week for a cash transaction, to six months. When I worked with bank-owned properties, a few took over a year, but those were complicated cases where individuals had intentionally clouded the title and lawyers had to decipher the mess. There were also issues with squatters, a subject that might warrant a book of its own.

If you're planning a 1031 Exchange, always keep your timelines in mind. The sellers won't care. We were once forced to back out of a property because the seller was taking too long. With our 180-day closing period expiring, we were past due diligence on two properties. On one of them, however, there was significant damage due to a storm and a large portion was condemned, meaning a loan wasn't possible.

Since we had no confidence in the seller, we put all the exchange funds into the first property and closed on that. We kept the other one under contract, but the seller delayed so long that we gave up. Looking back, the seller had attempted to strong-arm us into taking a hard money loan by deliberately dawdling on the repairs. They eventually sold it to another party, who a year later had the audacity to ask us to purchase the building for a huge profit. We told them to take a hike. You may think we could have gained by taking out a hard money loan to close, which is exactly what the seller had pushed for. As I mentioned before, we weren't confident in their repairs and wanted the threat of an appraiser to keep them somewhat honest. Instead, we used the funds to purchase two other buildings and made double the profit the new seller had asked for when remarketing the building, so in retrospect it all worked out. Last I heard, they're still searching for a buyer.

Coordinating with the Closing Parties

Closing a property is a bit like going to a dance. The main difference is you have a bunch of partners and you're all trying to coordinate your steps, so it resembles square dancing more than ballroom. Make sure there's someone calling out moves or every one of you will be lying on the floor and screaming from a broken ankle.

The parties necessary to make this happen include the lender, agent, escrow, closing attorney (not in all states), and title. A single person in that group can cause serious issues, so *do* take the advice of your lender and agent, whom you've already screened and verified to be trustworthy, and follow their recommendations.

This is the time to personally verify that all paperwork has been filled out correctly. You would be surprised how people in jobs that emphasize attention to details miss huge details. In one transaction, the bank tried to double the exit fee, a fee we couldn't avoid because this was a bridge loan and we were going to have to refinance later. In the same transaction, we were shell-shocked to see massive attorney fees. The bank provided an itemized list of expenses to justify their fees, and we noticed that many of the calls never happened. We provided phone call screenshots that verified two-minute conversations instead of two hours, and flight receipts proving we were in the air on the opposite side of the world at the time of at least one alleged call. When we threatened to bring these false charges to the state attorney's office, they offered a reduction in the fees, which we accepted.

Closing a deal for a commercial loan can be a shock to those coming from residential, primarily due to the significantly higher fees. In this arena you should rely on your agent and mortgage broker, who will help you ascertain what is reasonable and what is not. I've already outlined these expenses in Chapter 11.

Dealing with Bank Reserves

One expense you'll need to be prepared for is reserves. I covered these already but it's during this closing period that they're calculated exactly (the letter of intent will only contain estimates). These *are* negotiable but arguing that they're "too high" will get you nowhere. For repairs holdbacks, you'll need to provide expert opinions that the repair is either unnecessary or will cost less than their estimate.

At times, their estimator will attempt to be a general contractor. These people may not have seen your building, and it's unlikely that they have an in-depth understanding of building engineering or relevant state and local codes. In one instance, a bank demanded that we construct vents in the roof at significant expense. Our licensed and bonded general contractor investigated the claim and provided proof that what they prescribed would have violated the structural integrity of the building and, over time, would have led to its instability. He suggested a far cheaper alternative that would not cause such damage, and the bank accepted.

Chapter 17

Reviewing Expenses

Closing a building requires a careful balance of attention to costs and knowledge of the process. Concentrate on the big-ticket expenses. Honestly, if you see a two-hundred-dollar fee, it's not worth your breath to get bent out of shape over it unless there are several such fees. It's best to ask your mortgage broker what any unresolved expenses mean. You're looking out for the unreasonable expenses.

For example, at the time of writing this book, an appraisal shouldn't cost more than five or six thousand dollars on a fifty-unit apartment complex. If you see an appraisal costing ten thousand, then it's valid to question what caused this. How do you know what's a reasonable versus an unreasonable expense? Look at the lender's LOI, which contains estimates for all predicted expenses. If the actual expense is significantly higher, bring it up. There are banks out there who work with "special" partners who significantly overcharge, then provide kickbacks. You'll mostly find these on bridge loans and very small lenders. I haven't seen that from larger entities like Fannie and Freddie partners.

The big key when questioning these charges is to not be a jerk. Many charges are valid. Start by asking what this charge is for. In many cases, you'll only need an explanation. If the charge seems too high, do your homework to find out what it *should* be before you raise an issue. Always back up your disputes with data. Subjective statements will have no effect. For example, don't say, "This title fee is too much." You can say, "I closed on a nearly identical property two months ago, and this title fee is double that. Why?" Or you can say, "This title fee is triple what was on the LOI. Why?"

The Days Before Closing

Banks require a lot of paperwork and it's perfectly acceptable to be stressed out in the days leading up to closing. It's around this time that most of us dream of lying on a beach and relaxing. Please don't fly to some beautiful beach right before closing, then put your phone on mute and cash in on the unlimited drinks package. You're just asking for the closing to fail.

Lots of stuff happens two or three days before closing. I say "stuff" because it's mostly unpredictable. Maybe someone drove by and found an endangered jaguar with cubs in the crawl space. Maybe your property flooded.

More likely, your lender will need things at the last minute. They'll often ask for a rent roll, just to make sure the building is in the same shape financially right before closing. They may also ask for any new activity on your bank account. Most of the time the information required is easy to provide if you're still in the country and answering your phone.

Often, the loan documents don't reach escrow until one or two days before closing, and that's when discrepancies are found. Don't panic when this happens. That's why they're checked.

The day before closing, you'll sign a bunch of documents. I usually preview everything before that date, so the actual signing appointment moves quickly. The closing attorney will then notarize the documents, then overnight them to the bank.

At this time, funds are wired to escrow, who will provide the exact amount. This *isn't* the time to sell any stocks or mutual funds for the down payment. That should have been done well before. Do make sure to plan so you're not caught in a bad situation, waiting for funds to clear. This sounds obvious, but you'd be surprised how many people forget to do this.

The next morning, the bank will wire the remaining funds to escrow, at which point they'll release your deal to record in the appropriate county in your name. Normally, this is automatic, but snags can occur. I've already mentioned the case where the seller attempted to delay closing, hoping to reduce a yield maintenance fee, even though all funds had been wired. There was another deal where a last-minute title snafu also held things up. Problems happen, but they're rare.

Once the property has closed, transfer all utilities. I covered this in Chapter 15, but I'll mention it again in case you skipped that chapter. Escrow will only close out utilities capable of placing liens. They won't transfer any into your name. That's your job and if you fail to do this, the results could be very bad.

However, once all these tasks are completed, congratulations! You have a new property in your portfolio.

Chapter 18

The Value Add

THE BASIC PRINCIPLE of the value add is taking a building that looks like garbage, making it look better, and then raising the rents. The higher your rents are, the more the property is worth. Remember back to the Cap rate in Chapter 5. If the Cap rate is 5 percent and the building profits are $100,000 per year, then you can sell it for $2,000,000. If the rents are $150,000, then it's now worth $3,000,000.

What *Is* a Value Add?

In essence, a value-add is akin to printing your own money. Through your hard work, the income from rents increases, as does the property's value. The big difference is that if you actually print your own money, the government arrests you. If you instead do a value-add on a building, you get a tax credit. Both actions create money, but value-adds provide a nicer view from your room.

There are two basic parts to the value-add. First, you renovate the building.. Second, you raise the rents, because people pay more for nicer things. Where investors most often mess up in the val-

Chapter 18

ue-add is either renovating the wrong things or being too timid to raise the rents. We'll start with the renovations.

Contrary to popular stories, it's possible to put lipstick on a pig. You just need the right type of lipstick and a willing pig. A wig and cute hat also help. Similarly, a value-add doesn't usually involve tearing a building down to the studs, though it might. There's a common phrase in real estate, "The bones are good." This means that, even though the property might look horrid, the issues are mainly cosmetic. The electrical and plumbing are in fair condition, as are the framing and supports.

Typical Upgrades

These are the projects that cause a contractor's eyes to light up because he's about to hook up a vacuum to your bank account. Here are some typical upgrades:

> **Flooring** – I don't do carpet. It attracts allergens that can cause breathing problems. It also doesn't react well to pets and stains. Sure, it's cheap to lay down, but as nice as it looks on move-in, it will look abysmal on move-out. That's why I avoid it like the plague. Hardwood is also problematic. The top assumption you must make with all upgrades is that tenants won't take care of anything. It's just not wired into most people's heads to care for other people's stuff. That's especially true for hardwoods, which will be scratched and nicked to death.

Sure, some landlords require tenants to place area rugs and bill their security deposit for repairs, but resurfacing hardwoods can get pricy and generate fumes for neighbors, so it's best to not deal with it.

Luxury Vinyl Plank (LVP) flooring is usually the best choice. It's cheap and nearly indestructible. If something spills, the tenant just needs to wipe it off. Tenants *should* still put down an area rug, but the risk of scratches is far less. Of all the flooring I've used, LVP lasts the longest and looks the nicest after move-out.

Bathrooms – Showers are your mortal enemy. You're essentially letting water rush through the house with the hope that it doesn't seep into the walls and floors and rot the whole thing through. In my experience, tenants will never inform you that shower tiles need to be regrouted, or tell you about water damage. They'll wait until the tub crashes into the unit below them or a rat peeks out of the ceiling.

Do not even try to fight this battle. You'll never keep the tiles grouted and sealed. Instead, just buy a surround tub that's one piece. Then, you'll only need to keep an eye on the seal between the floor and the tub, which fails far less often and can be checked during inspections. Some of you may balk at this suggestion because such surrounds look cheap. Well, guess what? Your value-add isn't a palace and you're not living there. Besides, there are very nice surrounds out there these days. Some can even be painted.

Always replace the toilets. Older models flush more water than Niagara Falls and, in many buildings, you're paying for that. Newer toilets are cheap, so if you're doing any work in the bathroom, you should replace that toilet.

For the biggest bang for your buck, add a new vanity with lighting. Your contractor should have a relationship with a distributor of single-piece units that include the sink. Don't get too fancy with the faucets because tenants love to break them. Pick a standard type you know can be easily replaced.

Bathrooms are perhaps my favorite place in a value-add because for relatively little money you can make a dramatic change. Due to water damage, this is one room where you often have to rip things down to the studs and even replace a few. However, after you throw in a surround tub, redo the floors, and add a new vanity, the room will shine. The whole apartment will begin to look like something new.

Bedrooms – One thing to beware of when purchasing a building is small bedrooms. It's extremely difficult to make them bigger. When faced with smaller than average bedrooms, we've chosen not to buy. However, if the room is of average size, there's a lot you can do. Don't expect to fit in a king-sized bed, but you should be able to fit a double.

Besides the normal flooring and paint, you may want to add a ceiling fan. In the southern United States, fans are popular because people can run them instead of air conditioning, which uses more power and can be loud. You should also put in new blinds. Don't get fancy but do consider cordless options that can't become strangle traps for children.

One major upgrade you can at times carry out is converting a studio into a one-bedroom. Whether you can do this will depend on the layout and the local codes, but it can be an easy way to justify a bit more in rent. Look into "barndoors" to save space and position a closet as a divider. Again, the electrical, plumbing, or room layout may prevent this, but consider making this change where you have studios.

Lighting – Strongly consider changing your light fixtures throughout the unit. Often nice, stylish lights can be found for cheap at big box stores like Costco. It's especially important to change fixtures if they still use incandescent bulbs. Just replacing these will save you a bundle in electricity. Even if the tenant pays for power, new fixtures will look much better. When picking out bulbs, white lights are better than yellow ones for inducing good moods.

Electrical – To provide more contrast and freshness, consider replacing the outlets and light switches in a different shade than the wall covers. Make sure to buy ones that aren't easily breakable but are simple to remove. If they're not simple to remove, your painters might just paint right over them and then they'll be ugly again.

Electrical panels are a trickier issue. In certain cases, your bank may require you to replace one if it's old enough. Otherwise, discuss this with your inspector and general contractor. The main reasons to replace a panel are because it's old, has been recalled and is a fire hazard, codes require it, or you need more power. Otherwise, you're really spending money for no reason. Note that no tenant will ever walk into a building and say "Honey, we just *have* to rent here! They have a new panel!"

Doors and molding – Most of the time, you can repaint doors and molding. They only really need to be replaced if they have holes in them, though we've patched some up. If you must replace a handle, make sure to find one of a similar style so the unit doesn't appear thrown together.

Painting – I'd let you decide how do this yourself, but I've seen too many people screw it up. This isn't an opportunity to be artistic. Paint the doors, molding, and ceiling white. The rest of the unit you'll paint whatever's currently in style, but it should be a light earth tone. Light grey and beige have been popular recently. Please heed this advice. Potential tenants will run for their lives from an ugly apartment.

Kitchen cabinets – If they were built in the 1980s or later, then you can repaint them. In older buildings you're probably going to have to replace the entire cabinet structure because refacing will be too difficult. They could have also suffered from plumbing leaks and a lot of other issues and refinishing them may be an exercise in futility. If you do repaint, replace the handles as well. You'd be surprised how some paint and new handles and hardware will make cabinets look brand new.

Countertops – You don't always need to replace these, but when you do, consider Formica countertops that look like granite, or a thinner granite (three centimeters instead of four) that's imported. Granite countertops should be installed in A- and B-type units. Class C buildings won't pay for it.

Always choose a countertop that will take some abuse. We've installed butcher-block types for that purpose, since they last a long time even when mistreated.

Fighting Crime

Let's be honest. The reason many buildings are affordable is because the area sucks. Remember that your building is part of the reason the area is considered "bad" and that you actually have the power to do something about it. If your goal is to house quality paying tenants, then you're going to need to prove to them that your building is a safe place that justifies a higher rent. The following are ways to accomplish this.

Secure fencing – Criminals will often crisscross properties in order to avoid law enforcement. You can dissuade them from crossing onto your property by installing fencing across the non-public-facing boundaries. This needs to be robust fencing installed by a professional and it should ideally go below ground to discourage someone digging under it.

Cameras – Security cameras are a major way to prevent criminal activity from occurring on your property. Make sure the footage is monitored and to follow all local laws that cover disclosing the existence of the cameras and how the footage is handled.

Police patrols – If there's been an increase in criminal activity around your building, call the police department and request additional patrols. Often, they'll be happy to oblige.

Evictions – Ensure there's verbiage in your lease that allows you to evict for criminal activity or placing other tenants at risk. When you learn of such activity, do not wait for something to happen. Get rid of them, even though drug dealers and other criminals are often paying tenants. Work with your eviction attorney to ensure all laws are followed.

Enforce no extra guests – In my experience, the worst criminals are often not even on your lease. Because they have a criminal record, few landlords will rent to them, so they live with friends. A building 'snitch', as discussed in chapter 13, is a great way to know this is happening. Ensure that your lease stipulates this activity is forbidden and provide notice to the tenant when this occurs. Again, it's often better to evict than wait for something to go wrong,

All common areas are locked – Ensure that laundry rooms and any other common areas have doors that automatically shut and lock. Provide tenants with the key or passcode.

Value-Add Strategies

The general strategy with each value-add decision is to factor in that tenants will abuse whatever you install. You can try putting in nicer things and then deducting damage from the security deposit, but this just causes unnecessary stress. Put in components that are durable and hope they last a few tenants' turns.

Once you've decided what you'll do to the building, you'll have to figure out how to pay for it. There are two rough strategies.

First, you can use a lump sum at the outset to pay for them. Some banks will force you to do this, and they'll do so by requiring you to put the money aside in a holdback account they control. They'll release your holdback funds after you provide proof of the repairs. Of course, this requires that you have even *more* money at hand to pay for the actual repairs, but banks and common sense are rarely partners.

The second option is to use the money left over from rents. If you have two thousand left over after expenses and mortgage payments, then you'll do that amount of upgrades. This moves things at a slower pace, though as you renovate units and rent them out for more, you'll be able to afford more upgrades. In practice, I've found it takes twelve to eighteen months to completely turn a forty or fifty-unit building this way. The primary advantage is that you're not using up precious capital that could be used to purchase other buildings.

Exterior vs Interior Remodeling

Which should you improve first, the interior or the exterior? In my opinion, it should always be the interior. Think about it: if the interiors aren't habitable then it doesn't matter what the exteriors look like. Tenants are also far more tolerant with a dated exterior than a dilapidated interior. You should therefore always strive to improve the units before turning to beautifying the outside.

I've seen this bite a number of investors. One syndicate who owns a building near mine put a tremendous sum into making the exterior look gorgeous, then ran out of money. They're now stuck with a picture-perfect building that's uninhabitable. Another investor I know put a significant amount into the exterior, only for the interior to be condemned by the city. Focus on improving the units first, so tenants want to live there and are willing to pay more money, then turn your attention to outside improvements.

Whether you're renovating to improve your ROI or to increase the value of the building for sale, value-add is a crucial piece. Rarely should you pay top dollar for a property that's turn-key (which, in my opinion, doesn't exist). Instead, purchase something at somewhat of a discount and print your own money.

Chapter 19
Building Maintenance

Every building looked nice at one point. Then things like weather, tenants, and time took over and made them what they are today. Keeping your buildings in good condition is the difference between a well-oiled real estate machine and someone else's future value-add.

Keeping Track of Work

It can be difficult to keep track of what needs to be done, so I created a system. Each month I have a meeting with our property manager. The day before, I go over every unit we own. Tenants who are more than one month behind are marked as red, while those behind less than a month are marked as yellow.

The next day, at the meeting with our property manager, I go through the red units in order. This focuses the conversation, whereas before, the conversation ranged all over the place. I mostly ignore yellow units except as a total that indicates the general effectiveness of collections. Each tenant in red is also noted in a document where I enter by how much they're in arrears. Our property manager will then provide information about that tenant, and I'll add that to my notes. That way, when a tenant is late, I can easily see past behavior.

The reasons tenants are late vary. Often, they've already stopped in the office and alerted us to the fact and the staff is already working with them on a payment plan. Occasionally they're in the hospital. During the pandemic Covid was a common issue. Sometimes we have absolutely no reason. The tenant didn't pay and any attempt to reach him or her has failed. Based on this data, we'll choose whether to proceed to eviction.

After we've reviewed our problem tenants, we discuss the current state of repairs. What's preventing vacant units from being re-rented? Sometimes we're waiting on an inspector or appliance delivery and occasionally we've moved resources to another unit. I keep track of this status in my document, so for any unit, I can see the history of how work progressed.

Handling Evictions

Evictions are one of the tougher parts of being a landlord. You're going to have to do it at some point, and once you own enough units you'll still have to evict, no matter how well you screen people. While eviction evokes images of tossing starving families onto the street, the bitter truth is most of these are cases where renters have chosen to devote their money to other pursuits, instead of to their shelter. Sometimes due to their habits, local charities won't help them.

You also need to remember that you're running a business. The arrangement is simple: You provide shelter and keep it in order, and they pay you for it. A legal document exists that details the duties of both parties, and your tenant failed on his end. At this point, you must trigger an eviction and replace him with someone who pays.

It's important to have an eviction policy. It's between you and your property manager to decide when to evict. Even more important is that this policy needs to be the same for everyone. Your fairness should be evident in documentation, and it should be possible to go through all previous late tenants and see that eviction determinations were handled uniformly.

If you don't handle eviction decisions the same way for all tenants, you're asking for a lawsuit. Tenants talk and will be very curious why you let so-and-so off the hook when she was two months late, but not them. Below is one possible eviction policy.

If the tenant is less than a month late, contact them to determine the reason for the shortfall. If they're a month late, post a "seven day pay or vacate notice." Note that you should have a template already available so you can fill in the blanks. If you have a property manager, she can post it. Otherwise, you can post it, or—if you're scared of the tenant—eviction attorneys have services that can handle it for you. Make sure to check with your eviction attorney or local laws to follow eviction rules.

If the tenant is more than a month late, then your decision might depend on whether the tenant has communicated the circumstances. If your attempts at communication have failed, proceed to eviction. Otherwise, inform the tenants about government agencies and charities that can help them. Keep a list of such charities available for these situations. Call several beforehand to better familiarize yourself with their programs. If the tenant reaches two months late with no communication or progress, then proceed to eviction.

The eviction process varies from state to state, but in all states you should hire a lawyer to handle this. Each city has lawyers that only do evictions. Make sure to find one who specializes in this area of law, as a general-purpose lawyer will be far more expensive. The following rules for evictions apply in most states.

In the states where I've done business, we can't accept *any* money short of full payment once the eviction process is started. If the tenant gives us even ten dollars and we accept it, the process must start all over again. If the tenant attempts to partially pay, make it clear that you'll only accept a single payment consisting of everything owed.

Evictions for lack of payment are the easiest. Yes, most leases give other reasons, such as noise ordinances, smoking, and damaging the building, but these are much tougher to enforce. First, some cities prohibit evictions for these events. Second, the court case turns into a "he said, she said". Your legal costs might be significantly higher and the tenant could win with a spirited defense. Nonpayment is black and white. Either the tenant paid, or he didn't. The lease clearly states that the tenant must pay, so if he didn't, he's in violation.

Make sure to follow all local ordinances for evictions. For example, in the City of Seattle, it's illegal to evict in the winter. Therefore, your tenant can live rent-free from November to March. Pay attention to these limitations when purchasing a building. In many such communities, landlords raise rents to compensate for these losses, but verify that the ROI still makes sense before proceeding with the building purchase.

In my experience, tenants will usually vacate the unit before the case goes to court. In very rare cases we have needed a sheriff to be present. Note that in most cases the sheriff is there only for supervision. You'll need to hire someone to move the tenant's belongings to a storage unit or (in some states) outside to the parking lot. Many cities and states mandate for how long you must keep personal property in storage before you may dispose of it. Your eviction attorney should be able to guide you on what responsibilities you have.

Immediately after the tenant has vacated, or when the sheriff is overseeing a removal, bring a locksmith to the unit to rekey it. Tenants *will* try to reenter the unit, and if they're successful you may have to go through another eviction. This will depend on local ordinances and on how quickly you catch the squatters. We've unfortunately had cases where tenants broke in through a window and vandalized the unit. There's very little you can do in this case.

Even if you have security cameras that clearly show the vandal, police will generally do little more than file a report.

The easiest way to prevent squatters and vagrancy is to rent out the unit as quickly as possible. Sometimes this is difficult because there may be significant damage that requires repairs. Contractors are usually savvy enough to not leave their equipment overnight in a vacant unit. If contractors are at least making daily progress on the renovations, it will be hard for squatters to attempt possession. If this *does* happen, do not attempt to negotiate with them. Treat this as trespassing and report it immediately to the police. If you are self-managing the property, check on it once a day after an eviction, unless you have contractors there.

Evictions are an unfortunate side of the business. They force you to deal with the worst of society, though with proper screenings and a system to handle late tenants, you can minimize them. A more common concern is ensuring your building remains in good shape.

Building Maintenance

Over time, a small leak can turn into thousands or even tens of thousands of dollars in damage. It's your job as a landlord to ensure that doesn't occur. The easiest way to ensure that is to schedule quarterly or, at the most, semiannual inspections. Make sure your tenants are aware that you're not inspecting *them*. These are inspections to verify everything is working.

In the south, spray for pests monthly. In my experience, cockroaches never pay for lodging and annoy their neighbors. Similarly, tenants take unkindly to rats knocking on their bedroom door or raiding their fridge. Don't wait for an infestation. In areas where they're prevalent, service regularly.

In one of our properties, our contractor was inspecting units one day when he noticed something odd about the floor. It bounced up and down a bit. Since we didn't install trampolines in our units, this was concerning. Sure enough, when he investigated further, he found the sub-floor was completely rotten. While we had inspected the property before purchase, this had been missed.

We moved the tenant out of that unit to another we'd just finished renovating, then tore open the floors to find that the damage extended across the entire unit. When we found that the neighboring bedroom also had rotten floors, we ordered a full investigation for the entire building. Sure enough, a nearby unit had a water heater that had been leaking for years. We'd only owned the building for a few months, but the tenant had apparently never mentioned the problem to the previous owner, when it would have been easier to fix.

The repairs were significant since we had to move tenants out of the units with bad floors. Had we not begun regular inspections, we probably wouldn't have caught the issue until some poor tenant fell through the floor. The building was already a value-add project and, luckily, we had several vacancies. The affected tenants had no qualms about moving into newly renovated units. While we did find this issue through an inspection, the previous owner could have caught this problem far earlier, and fixed it for far less money, by simply running inspections themselves.

Dealing with Contractors

Once you encounter an issue, you'll have to deal with people called "contractors." Historically, contractors and owners have fought many battles and their disagreements are legend. While many believe the two groups cannot get along, that's a myth.

Building owners have long been frustrated when contractors perform shoddy work and take too long to complete a project. All too often a contractor will begin a job, then stall. Upon further investigation, the landlord will discover that the contractor has been working on another project and leaving hers in complete disarray.

Every contractor, for his part, has a story about an owner who didn't pay for a job, usually after the owner micromanaged every aspect of the project from when the workers showed up to the type of boots they wore. The owner fussed over every single thing, and when some trivial detail was missed, didn't pay him. Horror stories on both sides are why many owners and contractors don't trust each other. This doesn't need to be the case.

The key to a good relationship between owners and contractors is to treat each other as adults. On your part, there's no need to micromanage. You specify what work is necessary and the contractor owns completing it with good quality, at roughly the time specified, for approximately the initial estimate. The following principles will guide you towards achieving that.

Always pay the contractor on time. Many won't need a deposit once they trust you, but pay him immediately once the work is complete. This will move you way up on his priorities in future projects, too, because even owners who pay often take an obscenely long time to do so.

Don't concern yourself with what hours they work. As long as they're not keeping the entire building awake by running power saws at midnight, it doesn't matter when they're working. Install a contractor key box near the unit so they can enter whenever necessary. This also frees them to finish your project sooner, since they can fit it in around their schedule.

Don't tell them how to do their jobs. Even if you were once in the industry yourself, let them make that call. Respect them as experts and you should see a higher quality of work. What should you do if they mess up? If the work must meet local codes, you'll need to acquire a permit and pass an inspection. Contractors already understand that if an inspector requires them to redo work, then that's what needs to be done.

If you just don't like the quality, consider whether the tenants will have an issue. Don't be anal retentive about standard apartment repairs. Any change that could result in injury or death will require a city inspector, so you're covered there. At other times there may be no codes, but the work looks horrible, and you know a tenant will have issues. In that case, be polite and suggest that the contractor find a solution. I recommend you choose your battles and don't nitpick.

What to Expect with Contractors

I learned of one case where an investor went nuclear nitpick during a call with that investor. He'd recently had a new refrigerator installed in a unit. Even before he began his tirade, I wondered why he'd showed up for such an event. Honestly, this should be super simple. Tell the home improvement store to deliver the fridge, then call the tenant and verify there's a fridge. Problem solved. But no, the investor had to supervise the job personally.

Sure enough, the refrigerator arrived with three nicks. They were on the cabinet side, so no one would have ever seen them. As they took the fridge upstairs, one more ding appeared. He was livid. He called the manufacturer to complain about the dings, then called the store to complain about the delivery people. The manufacturer refunded him $100 and the store gave him another $80. He spent four hours on the phone arranging this, so he made $45 an hour. In the meantime, the deliverymen were rebuked and perhaps even charged for the dings, and no one is happier. This was simply not worth the investor's effort.

Sometimes your contractor is simply a moron. There are times when the quality of work done defies all common sense. If that happens, don't give him any more work. Don't yell or say you'll never work with him again because that may not be true. I've had contractors I "soft fired" and then called several years later and pretended he had worked for us yesterday. Why? Because it was an emergency and I couldn't find anyone else. Whatever you do, don't burn your bridges. If you don't like the quality of the work or the prices, just stop giving projects to him and find someone else.

Finally, don't expect a masterpiece. Your contractor isn't painting the Sistine Chapel on your ceiling, nor are millions of tourists going to stand in line to see it. The work should be clean and professional. That's it.

The strategies above will encourage contractors to get the job done, but you can do more. It's possible to get them to even *like* you.

Making Contractors Want to Work for You

The very best thing you can do is praise them for their work. Everyone loves to hear that they are appreciated. When a contractor finishes an urgent job, make sure to exclaim how lost you'd be without him (which isn't a lie) and thank him. When a unit is completely renovated and looks great, exclaim how amazing it is. Take a video. Make sure he knows you are showing how awesome his work is.

When contractors are working hard, feed them. Stop by and thank them for working so hard, then offer to pick up lunch. Alternatively, bring them coffee and cookies unannounced. While they'll likely interpret it as appreciation for their work, in truth you're bribing them. What do you want? You want them working on *your* projects, not someone else's. These little bribes will influence their future decisions. I also send gift cards for holidays. During a recent site visit, a contractor stopped to personally thank me for a gift card I'd sent nine months earlier. He said it meant a lot. I noticed he stayed late to finish a project, even though no one had asked him to.

Finally, don't negotiate on prices. Should you just accept what they offer? No. A good contractor will offer a fair price up front. If he instead gives an outlandish price, then don't use him. Sometimes contractors give high bids for projects they don't want, so keep him in mind for future work, but if you regularly hear ridiculous prices, then drop him further down your call list. Once you've worked with a contractor through several projects, you'll begin to trust each other for prices. You'll tell him what needs to be done, he'll provide a price, and you'll ask when he can start. At that point, you won't ask multiple contractors to quote the job. The entire discussion will take a few minutes. Depending on the nature of the work needed, you may even be able to show him a video of the job, so he can avoid a site visit.

In general, you should only obtain multiple bids for expensive jobs. A commercial roof is a prime example. They can easily run to tens of thousands of dollars, so you'll want to shop around. Do clarify *how* they're doing the work, though, because some contractors will bid higher because they're doing more. Before you say no to that extra work, do some research and ask him point-blank why this work is necessary. Sometimes it is, and sometimes it isn't. Often, it will depend on how long you want the work to last.

I learned the absolute worst way of hiring contractors from a colleague, who had the habit of inviting three contractors *at the same time* to examine the project and bid. He intentionally made sure they saw each other, with the expectation that the practice would make their bids more competitive. This is a lesson in failure, and indeed he constantly complained about problems with his contractors. The reason was obvious. Right off the bat, they hated him. I'm sure several bid high or just walked away. When you ask a contractor to show up and assess a project for bid, don't forget that you're taking his time. If he doesn't receive the work, he's wasted that time. Be nice and only bring in multiple contractors for expensive jobs. Even then, space them out. For small jobs, go from the top of your list, with the assumption that the first contractor you call will get the job if his price is reasonable.

Another horror story involved a fellow investor who called me to complain about a contractor not showing up. When I probed further, I learned that he'd painted the unit, then realized the carpet needed to be replaced. The investor called the contractor and was quoted a price. He then explained that the unit had just been painted, so the contractor would have to be sure not to create any dust when removing the old carpet, and would have to return the molding in exactly the same condition, since it had been painted too. The next day, the contractor called to say his car broke down. Then he was sick. Was he lying? Of course he was, but this investor couldn't expect to replace the carpet without requiring some touch ups on the paint.

If you follow my suggestions, contractors will learn that you're an easygoing person who appreciates their work, doesn't micromanage, feeds them, and pays on time. They'll want to work for you. Some will even show up on a Saturday afternoon when a bathroom is flooding and you have an emergency. If you build the right relationship, I promise that when you call and say jump, they will say how high. This is a lesson with all people. If you treat them right, you'll be treated well yourself.

Chapter 20

Figuring Stuff Out

THE PREVIOUS CHAPTER ends the "book" part of real estate investments. I hope I've answered your questions and provided you with a bit more. Those chapters provide a recipe for success. These final two are about not throwing that perfect recipe in the oven and burning it to a crisp.

You can know everything there is to know about real estate investment and still fail. In fact, the issues I've had to correct most often with my clients have required "soft" skills. First among them is the ability to figure things out.

The D-Method

My husband has a method he lives by called the "D-Method." He learned it in French class when his professor told a story about a transportation strike in Paris. On television, people were told by officials to use the "D-Method" to get to work. When Joe's professor inquired what that meant, she learned it stood for "débrouille-toi," which means "figure it out yourself."

The D-Method is very useful in real estate, as it enables you to resolve or mitigate all problems. You just need to apply it. The following are some examples where I've had to think on my feet. Your challenges will be different, but the process is the same.

The Case of the Mysterious Utility Pole

One afternoon during a rare snowstorm in our area, a utility pole decided it had had enough of life and tumbled, with power lines attached, onto my property's yard. There, after shaking the building up a bit, it sank into the snow amongst the quiet, since all civilization pauses in western Washington when snow arrives.

My tenants called me the moment it fell. It's common for tenants to panic and turn to you for help, even though they're perfectly aware you're not an emergency service. In this case, I did what they should have done. I called the fire department and asked them to determine if the wires were live.

They came right away and found that the wires weren't live. They speculated that it was cable or internet, and left. While the danger was over, I still had a large pole lying across my yard. It belonged to some utility company, but to whom? While the temptation was to just cut the wire and chop up the pole, I was concerned that utilities didn't just set up random poles in places. Although the wires weren't dangerous, they were still attached and were providing some service.

I asked my tenants to look for anything indicative on the pole, but they were too panicked, so I got in my car and drove down there. Sure enough, there was a small metal plaque with identifying information on the pole, declaring it belonged to the cable company.

That seemed simple enough. I called the cable company and gave them the identification number from the pole and asked them to put up a new one. After all, the pole itself was still a safety hazard and it had to be addressed. To my surprise, the woman on the line stated that it wasn't actually their pole. Since it was on my property, it belonged to me, and it was my job to replace it. She then hung up.

We were now five days into it and my patience was running low. Yet again, I called the cable company and this time I reached someone else. This time, I read the exact text on the pole that stated, "xxx numbers Name of Cable Company." I reiterated what their other representative had stated and calmly said that if the pole wasn't replaced by noon the next day, I would cut the wire and dispose of the pole. Then I hung up. This would remove service for the whole town and towns nearby. The ball was in their court and the choice was theirs, but I wasn't going to tolerate this pole endangering my tenants. At 9:00 a.m. the next morning their crew showed up, installed a new pole, and took the old one away.

Just because a company representative tells you something doesn't mean it's a fact. Be nice but stand your ground when you know you're right. Similarly, when others aren't getting something done and it's an emergency, do it yourself. Had I followed due process, that pole might *still* be sitting there. There probably would have been a few lawsuits, too, from people tripping over it.

The Vent over the Granite Island

This next story is from one of my rare flips. The kitchen remodel was simple. I added a nice island with granite countertops and had ducting installed for an overhead vent. The space was tight and there was only one model of vent that would fit in that spot. I had a general contractor for the job and it was his responsibility to procure all appliances and materials on time. I learned from this project that he wasn't the brightest tool in the shed.

I'd already had to (with kindness) request that he undo the drywall he'd placed over every outlet in the kitchen, so I wasn't greatly surprised when he called to state that the project would be delayed three weeks because he couldn't procure the vent. It had been in stock a week ago, but now was sold out. Every project in the house would be completed on time, except for the vent. He'd already talked to the home improvement store, and they placed it on backorder and gave him the three-week estimate.

There were multiple issues with this. Since I had a hard money loan, a three-week delay meant another interest payment. It also put me perilously close to the end of the loan when I factored in market and closing time, and so I would have to pay another point or so to extend it. Everything had been planned according to a timeline, and in order to meet mine the property needed to be listed within forty-eight hours. I couldn't list it with a huge hole in the kitchen ceiling, nor could I photograph it without that vent in place.

I got on the phone and called every home improvement center in Puget Sound (nowadays this search is much easier to accomplish online). I soon found a store that had my vent and promptly gave them our credit card to purchase it.

Within an hour of our telephone conversation, I gave the contractor the address of the store and asked him to pick it up. By the same morning, the vent was installed. That same afternoon, the home was photographed and then listed, on time, the next day.

Understand that others working with you don't have the same priorities. This contractor didn't have a hard money loan to pay. He didn't have such specific deadlines. When the deadline is on *you*, it's *your* responsibility to meet it. That may mean getting on the phone to figure things out. You can *ask* others to help, but when it's your butt on the line, be prepared to step into the action yourself to make things happen.

Journey to the Center of the Parking Lot

One evening, while our building and its tenants were peacefully going about their business, the earth opened and a section of our parking lot descended into the depths of hell. We had a sinkhole. In this case, the tenants called the police instead of me. However, since the officers were unable to arrest the sinkhole, nor would it vacate the premises, they called me.

I couldn't recall a section on sinkholes in my real estate primer, so I admit I was at a loss on what to do, but the first step was obvious; I immediately had my contractor build a barrier around it to ensure no one fell in. That delayed a lawsuit but we still had a huge hole in the center of our parking lot. Would it get bigger? How could we resolve this?

I called my insurance company. He said that there was probably something they could do, but he also admitted that this was his first experience with a sinkhole. I couldn't wait for him to look up a procedure. I had to know if I was about to own a subterranean apartment complex. After a bit of research, the next day I called the city.

Even though this was completely on my property, it's always in the city's best interest to ascertain whether portions of it are about to collapse into oblivion. They promptly sent engineers to investigate the matter and determined that it was not about to expand. Further, they gave me permission to fill it.

Since filling the sinkhole could be expensive, I asked my property manager to obtain several quotes. However, given the seriousness of the matter, I did my own research to understand exactly how to fill a sinkhole. That led me to discover a local company that specialized in sinkholes, so I requested that my property manager call them. This was a project that needed to be done right. If an unknowing contractor threw the wrong materials down there, the problem would become worse.

Again, when the problem is serious, get involved and figure things out. Remember that this is *your* responsibility. If someone fell down that sinkhole, I would have been sued. When there's an emergency affecting your building or tenants, it's your job - and your job only - to ensure it's resolved. This usually means hiring the right professionals to resolve it, but you still own making sure it gets done. The squeamish may wish to skip my next example.

Chapter 20

The War of the Rental Units

In some cities the cockroaches grow so large that it's necessary to obtain hunting licenses to take them down. The bugs are nearly indestructible and I'm beginning to wonder if they're the ones running the laundry services. In the story I'm telling you now, I had several units we couldn't rent due to constant cockroach parties.

Each time my property manager sent pest control to fog them, the parties kept getting larger and larger. The problem became so severe that tenants were leaving. There was a silver lining in that I could now renovate those units and charge more, but not until the cockroaches were evicted. However, no matter how many times pest control served pay-or-vacate notices, the cockroaches remained.

Clearly there was another problem. While I'm sure the fog bombs were obliterating a few, there was another source. I told my property manager to stop calling pest control, since clearly that wasn't working.

Again, I turned to my friendly search engine and enrolled in a course on cockroachology. These vermin need a food source to stay alive. Since we'd removed any such source from the now-vacant units, there had to be some other food source. After some more research, I learned that cockroaches often survive in pipes with leaks.

May I say again how happy I am to have contractors? Armed with this knowledge, I sent one under the crawl space to investigate, and sure enough he found a pipe with a hairline crack. Surrounding it was a population of cockroaches the size of Manhattan. I couldn't even look at the photos.

Another call to the plumber fixed the crack, and then we called pest control back in to annihilate the now-starving creatures. And… that's how you solve problems.

The lesson from my examples is that if you want to succeed in this business, you're going to need to figure things out. Don't panic, even when things seem dire. Remember that *you* chose this profession, so it's on *you* to solve the problem. If you sit and wait for things to happen, they won't. In the meantime, your tenants will grow angrier and all the goodwill you've worked toward in that building will be gone.

I've stuck to my own stories here, but I've seen many cases where someone purchased a wonderfully profitable building, hired all the right people, and then screwed it up because a problem occurred and they mishandled it. Don't be that person. Roll up your sleeves and get it done, without complaining, without yelling, and with minimal drama. Will you be stressed? Yes. And that's the subject of my final chapter.

Chapter 21

Mental State

I DON'T WANT to scare you but if you grow large enough in this industry, you'll eventually have a nervous breakdown. I've had a few and pretty much every investor I know has been through some. It's not always just the real estate. Family drama has a way of occurring at the exact same moment as property drama, and I can't call a contractor to fix the family situation.

I don't know if it was being still locked up for Covid, or a tenant killing himself, or the stress of purchasing a building during Covid that made banks triple the amount of paperwork, or the fact that a child molester was arrested in my building along with the child's parents who were knowingly selling their child, but the combined mass brought me to a nervous breakdown.

Two days later, I bought flight tickets and checked myself into a resort called Miraval in Austin. The resort focuses on the mind, body, and soul, which was obviously what I needed. I recall sitting outside the yoga barn and listening to soft spa music playing in the background while I watched a butterfly and a dragonfly flicker their wings. I suddenly burst into tears with the realization that I'd been moving a thousand miles an hour and had forgotten how to slow down and be in the present.

The next morning, during a guided meditation session, my mind was again moving at a thousand miles an hour over every bit of drama that had happened. Toward the end of the session, the instructor used Tibetan bowls to create some sound and suddenly I felt a sharp pain in my left ear, as if someone was twisting a knife there. Something just didn't feel right. I told myself that the only way to overcome it was to just let go. I just kept repeating, "Let go. Just let go" and I felt the huge pain let go. The sound of the Tibetan bowls then traveled around the room into my right ear and out my left side.

That was the day I realized I can't control everything. Depression can come from things that happened to us in the past. Anxiety kicks in when we anticipate something that's going to happen to us in the future. Being present in the moment was the only state where my mind, body, and soul were at peace. It's okay to let go.

If you want to survive, and I don't mean just in this industry, you need to take care of your mental well-being. We can only take so much abuse. Even when your properties are humming along perfectly, things happen. Every one of us will undergo drama in our lifetimes.

For me, vacations are my way to escape. I travel with my husband at least once or twice a year to some peaceful location. Recently, we travelled to Africa. There's nothing as serene as having a sundowner at a savannah or watching an elephant family drink at a watering hole and have a mud bath. We also travel to Europe and focus on the experiences as much as the destinations. I've taken cooking classes in Marrakech, Morocco, and Matera, Italy. I've enjoyed champagne tasting in Champagne, France, and ridden camels in Dubai. I even rode an ostrich in South Africa, though I wouldn't recommend that.

Investing in real estate can be both fun and stressful. Personally, I experience more of the former than the latter, but the final step towards mental health is knowing your exit strategy. How much do you need to earn from your properties to call it quits? Take a serious look at your expenses and come up with a number.

Given the current ROIs on your buildings, how many more investments do you need to reach that? How will you purchase those properties? Short of winning the lottery, there are two ways to reach your financial goals. You can either save the profits from rents, or you can sell a smaller building and purchase a larger one. I do both.

However, I don't think your goal should be to just keep expanding. At some point, you'll have enough. Sit down and calculate when you'll be there. Circle the date on your calendar or create a reminder on your phone since no one has paper calendars anymore. In the meantime, invest in yourself. Enjoy the beauty around you. It's okay to let go and just be.

Are there other financial goals you want to meet with your properties? Real estate investment is a great way to pay for a child's college. You may also choose to sell further down the line to finance that business you've always dreamed of. Most of us will never be featured on *The Lives of the Rich and Famous* but many of us can still live comfortably.

The knowledge that your retirement will be possible at a young age, and that it will free you to do what you want, should ease your mind. There's nothing more exciting than the realization that you can accomplish your goals. You're on that path towards a future where you can focus on what you truly love. What do you truly want to do? Maybe you'll write a book. Maybe you'll get into photography or painting. The world awaits your talents. I've only shown you the door.

www.ingramcontent.com/pod-product-compliance
Lightning Source LLC
Chambersburg PA
CBHW071232080526
44587CB00013BA/1579